Collab   Velfare

of related interest

Collaboration in Social Work Practice
Edited by Jenny Weinstein, Colin Whittington and Tony Leiba
ISBN 1 84310 092 4

Developing Good Practice in Community Care
Partnership and Participation
Edited by Vicky White and John Harris
ISBN 1 85302 890 8

Relational Social Work
Toward Networking and Societal Practices
Fabio Folgheraiter
Translated by Adrian Belton
ISBN 1 84310 191 2

Integrating Care for Older People
New Care for Old - A Systems Approach
Christopher Foote and Christine Stanners
ISBN 1 84310 010 X

The Changing Role of Social Care
Edited by Bob Hudson
ISBN 1 85302 752 9

Collaboration in Health and Welfare

Working with Difference

Ann Loxley

Jessica Kingsley Publishers
London and Philadelphia

First published in the United Kingdom in 1997 by
by Jessica Kingsley Publishers
116 Pentonville Road
London N1 9JB, UK
and
400 Market Street, Suite 400
Philadelphia, PA 19106, USA

www.jkp.com

Copyright © Ann Loxley 1997
Printed digitally since 2005

Library of Congress Cataloging in Publication Data
A CIP catalog record for this book is available from the Library of Congress

British Library Cataloguing in Publication Data
Loxley, Ann
Collaboration in health and welfare : working with difference
1. Health services administration 2.Public welfare administration
I.Title
362.1

ISBN-13: 978 1 85302 394 1
ISBN-10: 1 85302 394 9

Contents

Acknowledgments

I should like to thank Professor Geoff Pearson for facing me with the original question, 'what is collaboration?'; Dr June Huntington for guidance at the beginning; Professor Hugh Barr, Dr Rita Goble, Dr John Horder and Ms Lonica Vanclay for reading and commenting upon drafts; the King's Fund Library for unfailing helpfulness; colleagues on the Council at The Centre for the Advancement of Interprofessional Education for stimulation and ideas; Mrs Linda Clark of Enfield and Mrs Jean Thompson of Lincoln for typing and setting out; my first consciously interprofessional collaborators, Ms Judith Bryant, Dr Michael Carmi and Ms Valerie Packer; and the National Institute of Social Work, where this book began.

And finally my family for their interest and my husband Ronald for all his encouragement.

Preface

This book is written about collaboration, not to celebrate it, nor to exhort professionals to practise it, but to demystify it. Key ideas are drawn from a critical analysis of the concept of collaboration in the hope that educators, practitioners and managers in health and social care will be able to use these ideas when interprofessional and interagency collaboration is considered necessary.

The analysis is not an academic exposition, but an understanding for action. It is written by an actor for actors. It is based upon reflection on practice in a variety of roles; as a medical social worker in teaching and general hospitals; as an educator on generic social work courses in a major polytechnic, where students were supervised in a wide range of community-based settings, and where knowledge for practice was drawn from the social and human sciences; as a manager in a faculty of social science, and a networker on behalf of that faculty with five schools of nursing in the setting up of qualifying courses; as a policy-maker at a local level through membership of a district health authority; as an organiser and teacher on interprofessional courses with a general practitioner and a health visitor; and as a founder member and trustee of the Centre for the Advancement of Interprofessional Education. Collaboration has been a major element in these experiences which have been set in the changeable worlds of health and welfare since the early 1970s.

The difficulties of collaboration have been well documented, but as a strategy and as a policy, it also faces external threat. Professions are at risk of deregulation and fragmentation by governments seeking to weaken alternative bases for power. In the ostensible search for efficiency and cost effectiveness policy-makers promote proposals for core skills among professions, even for a core worker or a generic therapist. Current employment needs determine relevant training. On-the-job training, it is argued by politicians, is more effective than education in an academic setting. The purchaser/provider split in both health and welfare fragments and frustrates the professional task by separating assessment from response.

The case for interprofessional collaboration in health and welfare needs to be defended and actively promoted if generic care is to benefit from all the specialist knowledge and skills which have grown up in theory and practice in the fields of medicine, nursing, social work, occupational therapy and physiotherapy, to name only some of the possible players. Changes in policy are taking place so fast that professions need to respond quickly if they are to demonstrate that they are capable of providing generic care together.

To do this, collaboration must be disentangled from a muddle of belief, strategies and skills and from the suspicion of those afraid of losing autonomy, so that it can be widely understood, the necessary structures can be put in place, and the essential skills learnt and applied. If this can be done, collaborative effort can be explicitly purposeful, the necessary resources claimed and the outcome evaluated against the agreed intention.

My experience has been that interprofessional and interagency collaboration is, despite the difficulties, creative and exciting. In examining the concept of collaboration more critically, I hope to make its practice more possible.

Introduction

The word 'collaboration' rather than 'co-operation' has been chosen although both mean working together, because it carries implications of the enemy, of the other, to be regarded with some suspicion. Conflict is interwoven with interprofessional collaboration because there are deep-rooted social differences in the division of labour which has developed over the last 200 years in the health and welfare services. There are differences of knowledge, of ways of working, of priorities. There is competition for resources and for power among professions. Collaboration is not experienced as easy. It is, however, recognised as sometimes necessary in meeting the complex needs of individual patients or clients, or responding to complex social problems.

Working together, or choosing not to work together, will always be based on certain assumptions about the needs to be met, the relevance of other professions and their contribution, the costs involved, and the likely results. Such assumptions are not usually spelt out. But if collaboration, working with different others, is to be purposeful and defensible, then the assumptions on which it is based must be made explicit so that they may be critically examined, and people may be accountable for their work and its costs and benefits. Practice cannot be left to make sense of itself. It needs to have a dialogue with theory, to create models and frameworks which are coherent and consistent, challenge-able and testable, and transferable to similar situations at a different time or place.

Collaboration in health and welfare does not exist in isolated acts between autonomous professionals. It takes place between people who work in organi-sations small or large, and generally draws on public resources. Collaboration is determined by the diverse ways in which peoples' needs are defined and understood in society. It is seen as a means to a variety of ends, whether to meet the needs of the whole person, to achieve economies in the use of resources, or to bridge the gap between the health services and the welfare services. To be effective it depends on particular skills, structures and ways of organising and managing work.

Before it is possible to set out a framework for collaboration describing the skills and conditions required to organise it successfully, it is necessary to explore the idea of collaboration itself. The exploration travels through the context of collaboration in public policy and in the developments in health and social care which have affected its development. Some theoretical approaches to social interaction are examined for their relevance to the idea of collaboration, to see how they might illuminate it from outside. The difficulties so often documented in accounts of collaboration are related to sociological concepts of power, culture and structures to discover the social influences which affect attempts to work together and to find out what the professions might share as well as what divides them. These strands are then brought together to create a framework for the structure and process of collaboration which incorporates the difficulties and suggests the necessary skills to address them.

Chapter One describes the context for collaboration in health and welfare and examines the social policies and developments which affect it and the purposes it is expected to achieve. The practice and promotion of collaboration cannot be ahistorical or apolitical because it does not take place in a vacuum but in social arenas where resources have to be won and where it is wise to be aware what use is being made of the idea, and what interests are being served.

Chapter Two tries to analyse what collaboration involves, and how it may be illuminated by drawing upon theoretical ideas about social behaviour and examining possible assumptions underlying social interaction. Social theories and reflection on practice are used to try and understand the complexities of interprofessional collaboration, and what might affect its success or failure. The use of social sciences as a tool for understanding an idea like collaboration which is shared by several professions illustrates the difficulties actually being addressed. The problem is that the social sciences explore society from perspectives and with concepts unfamiliar to many clinicians, although they are increasingly part of the education of nurses and therapists, as they have always been part of the education and training of social workers. If, however, the use of social theories can enrich practice which all professionals share, then that enrichment is enough reason to accept the use of relevant theories, even though their ideas and language may not be held in common. The diversity of knowledge is to be used as a resource, offered and accepted as part of the trust which is an essential element of fruitful social interaction.

To avoid the suggestion that collaboration is always desirable, Chapter Three sets out some criticisms of interprofessional collaboration, especially in relation to its costs, and to examining whose interests it serves. Collaboration is not a universal panacea, nor is it cheap, though it must be efficient if it is to be justified. Understanding its costs tempers enthusiasm with reality.

Chapter Four examines the context of collaboration not from the external setting as in Chapter One, but through the factors which are inherent in the division of labour in health and welfare, which has developed through the pursuit of specialist knowledge and skills and been reinforced by the organisation of services. The more complex the division of labour, the greater is the interdependence of professions and agencies, but the differences and difficulties have their roots deep in society, and need to be understood if they are to be disarmed and used. This section also examines four major movements in the interprofessional response to collaboration and its difficulties: the growth of organisations to foster and promote collaboration; the emphasis on teamwork, especially in primary health care; the spread of interprofessional education, largely at post-qualifying level and as part of continuing education; and the search for theory in the growing body of publications.

Chapter Five attempts to set out a theoretical framework for collaborative practice and education which does not duck questions of structure or resources, nor pretend that it is purely a pragmatic, instrumental technique. The understanding put forward has a moral component which emerges from the interaction of theory and practice. Skills are identified which relate to context and theory, some of which have been applied in the development of the framework; that is, reframing perceptions, mapping contexts, building structures; managing through skills and evaluating outcomes complete the process.

The conclusion draws the threads together and explores questions of values in interprofessional collaboration. The aim has been to enable practitioners, educators, managers and policy-makers to move beyond description of collaboration into analysis and evaluation in its own terms. It is argued that interprofessional and interagency collaboration must become an activity which can be reliably prescribed when it is judged necessary for effective service. Collaboration should not be a panacea, nor an article of faith, nor dependent on haphazard circumstances, but a taught and resourced part of each profession's repertoire of skills, organisation, and culture.

CHAPTER ONE

Public Policy and the Context of Collaboration

This chapter outlines some social changes in the second half of the 20th century and the ways in which they have affected the organisation of health and welfare provision. It argues that the need for co-ordination between health and welfare services has been recognised in public policy which formally requires professionals and agencies to work in partnership. The purposes of collaboration in policy documents are threefold: to meet the needs of the whole person, to bridge the gap between the organisation of health care and the organisation of welfare, and to achieve economies in the use of limited resources. An understanding of what makes collaboration possible is evolving slowly. The context is one of continual change in philosophies, policies and organisation.

Introduction

Concern for the welfare of the sick and needy has been expressed through public policies since the Elizabethan Poor Law Act in 1598, which remained the basis of provision for over 300 years. Public health measures developed from the 19th century within the growing complexity of local government, while personal health care depended on a range of public, voluntary and private provision.

The first half of the 20th century saw in the western industrialised world an enormous development in biomedical knowledge and technology, which interacted with a focus on disease and a concentration on acute medicine. The associated prestige supported the growth of a dominant medical profession increasingly subdivided into specialisms and powerful enough to affect public policy. The emphasis in hospitals changed from the care of the poor to the aspirations of scientific medicine. The tensions between developing specialisms and the need for integrated care continued to grow.

In the period between the two World Wars and during the Second World War it became clear that adequate health services could not be maintained without a change in organisation and funding. The National Health Service Act 1946, rejecting the earlier proposals for a unified health service based on local government because of opposition from the medical profession and on the grounds that funding needed to be national and local authorities were too small, set up a tripartite structure of hospital and specialist services, the general practitioner service, and the local authority health services. Health and welfare crossed the organisational divisions, because in the local authorities the Medical Officer of Health was responsible for public health and community services, and the NHS hospitals employed their own social workers, the hospital almoners, later medical social workers and psychiatric social workers.

The organisation, financing, managing and provision of both health and welfare care since the mid 1970s has been subject to more and accelerated change than in the first 25 years following the inception of the NHS and the beginnings of the Welfare State. Social and economic pressures and changing political philosophies have impinged upon taken-for-granted assumptions, and called into question accepted beliefs in the face of conflict and contradictory demands. At the highest level of generality the goal of healthy members of a healthy society is likely to be agreed. The questions are then ones of definition, strategies and methods, among which collaboration is one.

Since the middle of the century different currents in society have interacted to bring about changes in the provision and organisation of health and welfare. Demand has risen and changed, and at the same time it has become apparent that while demand is open-ended, resources are limited. Political ideas about what is desirable and how it might be achieved have altered. Techniques in medical care have developed as new procedures have evolved. There have been challenges to the dominance of the medical profession, both from philosophers and from the rise of new aspirant professions. Changes in the organisation and management of health and welfare have resulted from the search for efficiency and value for money.

Threading through many of these changes have been tensions which reflect different values in society. These tensions affect directly the ways in which different agencies and different professions are able to work together.

Changing demands on health and welfare services

Demographic

A major pressure arises from the increasing number of people living for longer, true not only in this country, but for Western Europe as a whole. In 1971 just over 13 per cent of the population of the United Kingdom were aged 65 or over. This proportion is projected to rise to 15.7 per cent in 2001, 16.6 per cent in 2011 and 19.4 per cent in 2021. The age group which is likely to make the greatest demand on health and welfare services is those over 80 years. The proportion of this age group within the total population is projected to more than double between 1993 at just under 4 per cent and 2051 with just over 9 per cent, a result of the baby-boom of the 1960s and increased longevity. (HMSO 1996).

It is nearly 13 times as expensive to provide health care for people over 85 years as for those between 5–64 and the NHS expenditure on services for the elderly is increasing faster than health spending in general (PSI 1991). Moreover, these elderly people are not traditional recipients of welfare, but span the whole economic and social class range of society, and therefore bring expectations of health and social provision which are not likely to be easily satisfied by a poor-grade service.

Expectations

Expectations of health and social care, far from diminishing as was confidently expected 50 years ago with the advent of a National Health Service and the Welfare State, have continued to grow. Developments in medical knowledge, treatment and technology have contributed to the rise in expectations. If it is possible to develop and carry out a new procedure successfully, demand increases and it becomes difficult to argue on other than economic grounds that it should not be widely available. Doctors and patients have become socialised to expect State of the Art medicine.

Alongside these developments has run political concern about cost containment, carried out through a variety of mechanisms, from budgetary control through cash limits to competition in internal markets. The public wants effective use of resources in the face of rising demand, with adequate resources to meet needs. Stories of emergency patients ferried miles in search of intensive care beds do not witness to either effectiveness or adequacy.

In theory patients and clients have become consumers, with their purchasing power exercised through general practitioners and care managers as agents. The power to complain if expectations are not met, even to litigate, has become more acceptable. Users are now a force to be taken seriously.

A further pressure on resources arises from the growth of self-help pressure groups, especially where illness such as cancer has a high public visibility and arouses anxiety. The recognition of social problems, for example non-accidental injury to children, Aids and drug abuse, has called for contributions from health and welfare services, as well as from other professionals such as teachers and the police, and the expected response is not only that professionals should play their separate parts, but that they should co-ordinate their efforts. The challenges to professional autonomy are strengthened by budgetary controls as well as by political shifts to managerialism, by the increasing expectations of consumerism and the contribution of the voluntary sector.

As the incidence of contagious disease and diseases of deprivation has fallen, so the incidence of diseases of affluence, for example alcoholism, obesity, the consequences of road traffic accidents and stress-related diseases, has risen. Some conditions are therefore being presented as partly self-inflicted and consequently avoidable. Responsibility is laid on individuals to manage the maintenance of their own health, through lifestyle measures such as diet, exercise, promoted through journalism and even supermarkets. For some of the population, however, poverty makes it impossible to participate and the diseases of deprivation threaten to reappear. Whatever the popularity of lifestyle measures, ageing cannot be indefinitely postponed. With the ageing of the population has come an increase in degenerative conditions which affect mobility, communication and independence and which therefore require responses from family and health and welfare services which need to be managed and co-ordinated.

Changing philosophies

As changes have taken place in knowledge and technology, in the age spread of populations and in the incidence of diseases, and in perceptions of how need might be met, so also the social and political context within which health and welfare services are set has changed. Such change takes place as a result of struggles for power over what is to be pursued as desirable, and over how the pursuit is to be organised and resourced.

The NHS itself was a manifestation of the 19th-century legacy of the hope of infinite progress. It was intended not only to supply universally and free at the point of service the benefits of modern medicine, but was also seen to express desirable values in society. In the words of Richard Titmuss (1970), the NHS, 'the most unsordid act of British Social Policy... has allowed and encouraged sentiments of altruism, reciprocity and social duty'. These hopes of social reform and the pursuit of social justice through welfarism and universalism had their last expression in the setting up of the large local authority Social Services Departments in 1970 following the Seebohm Report of 1968.

The findings of the Black Report in 1980 (Townsend and Davidson 1982) showed that poorer members of the community and poorer parts of the country benefited least from the NHS and that social class was a major determinant of the gain to individuals. Welfarism and universalism in the provision of social goods could no longer be unquestioned. The challenge came first on the grounds of cost, and then the ideals of Beveridge and Titmuss were attacked politically from the radical Right. The political consensus on the givenness of collective provision as a means of distributing health and welfare benefits broke.

The emphasis moved from co-ordination to competition and from altruism and reciprocity as funding principles to a philosophy emphasising individuals as consumers, providers of services as entrepreneurs, and the market as a governing principle.

Medicine too has come under increasing attack. Philosophers such as Illich (1976) argued against the medicalisation of social issues. Marxist critics like Navarro contended that the system of health care was inextricably bound to and reflected the aims and needs of capitalism. Public health doctors (McKeown 1976) suggested that medicine played only a minor role in determining the health of the population.

The development of the Social Sciences as an academic discipline encouraged the questioning of taken-for-granted assumptions about, for example, the rise of professions. Friedson (1970) eloquently attacked the professionalisation of medicine. He wrote: 'Consulting professions... are well-meaning groups protected from the public by organised autonomy... of the inherently superior qualities of themselves as professionals... It is time that their autonomy be tempered'.

Professions, particularly dominant ones like medicine, but also developing ones like social work, could no longer uncritically be assumed to be benevolent experts, but might also be seen as self-interested players.

A further challenge to the predominance of hospital-based acute medical services came from the World Health Organisation. It has emphasised the importance of planning and organising for prevention of illness and health promotion through multi-sectoral co-ordination of social programmes. It has advocated a policy of primary health care, responsive and close to the needs of local communities. In the UK these proposals influenced policies emphasising the needs of designated priority groups – elderly, mentally ill and mentally impaired people and children, traditionally Cinderella groups in medical organisation, and later the development first of the idea of community care and then of its organisation and practice. Primary health care has become the domain of general practitioners, augmented by the Primary Health Care team.

Changing patterns of health and welfare

The organisation of care has developed in two distinct ways in response to and as part of changes and pressures in wider society. On the one hand there is the growth in high technology medical intervention, dependent on an expensive and complex support system, but able to effect in instances dramatic cures which would have been unimaginable two generations ago. At the same time in primary health care there has been a qualitative change in the selection and training of the generalist practitioner, working from a relatively cheap base in growing co-operation with other care professionals and serving a local population. These two distinct movements, both influenced by the search for specialisation, rest on two distinct models of intervention, the one an acute episodic model of cure and the other a long-term maintenance model of care. These two models arise from the changes in patterns of morbidity in western developed society. The shift from diseases of deprivation to diseases of affluence and degeneration brings an emphasis not only on life itself but also on the quality of life.

The growing professionalisation and the move into higher education of social work, nursing and the physical and psychiatric therapies have enabled these occupational groups to mount a challenge to the earlier pervasiveness of a medical model of care. The shift to a maintenance model, with its emphasis on the management and co-ordination of many different elements of health and social well-being over a period of time, has complemented the recognition of the bio-psycho-social interaction in the understanding of the whole person as a basis for action. In rehabilitation and in therapeutic communities, the idea of the collaborative team has developed, in responding to complex situations where the needs of individuals and families cannot satisfactorily be met by one occupation or one agency working in isolation.

So on the one hand there are the high technology medical specialists working on an essentially reductionist view of man but dependent on a complex, expensive network of support systems, and the generalist practitioners increasingly recognising a holistic view of human beings which demands an interprofessional and collaborative response.

Opposing tensions in the organisation of both health and welfare

In order to understand the social context in which collaboration may or may not be possible or desirable, it is useful to identify opposing tensions in the organisation, finance, management and goals of Health and Social Services and to recognise that such tensions are common to both.

Care versus cure

The emphasis on cure as the legitimate and sometimes the only goal of medicine, especially acute medicine, and the associated styles of treatment, has distorted the recognition of care as being of equal importance. The two goals have been traditionally separated, with higher status and greater power attached to the professionals who are expected to produce cures, and low status, even stigma, not only for the patients but also for the practitioners who offer care. These differences are reflected also in the allocation and reallocation of resources. A parallel division is apparent in the organisation of social work, where crisis intervention in the control and care of 'problem' families with children at risk takes precedence in the allocation of skilled resources over the long-term care needs of elderly and disabled people, client groups who are often lumped together with little formal recognition of their differing needs.

The division between cure or control and care is a false perception. Care and cure are part of a continuum in the achievement of health and welfare on an individual and at a community level.

Central versus local control

The increasing tendency toward central control over funding and policies is intended partly to contain public expenditure, and partly to establish fair and standard provision. At the same time there is a conflicting policy goal of putting operational and financial decision-making to the local level, to be responsive to local conditions and to encourage local responsibility and involvement. The result is that budgets are spent locally, with limited local autonomy, but are allocated and capped centrally. These two opposing forces can interact to create mutual distrust and low morale.

Bureaucratic or collegiate structures

The structures of the NHS and the local authority social service departments are hierarchical and bureaucratic, and have consequent styles and procedures of decision-making and the allocation of responsibility. Professions emphasise the importance of the collegiate peer group, and of professional autonomy and discretion. Their values assume the allocation of resources for the benefit of the individual patient or client. The discrepancy between professional expectations and the employing organisation leads to discomfort which is experienced especially by social workers and increasingly by hospital doctors. The devolution of budgets to fund-holding general practices has meant a greater emphasis on administration and management which strains the traditional collegiate structure.

Dominance by professionals or by managers

These tensions are characteristic of all health care systems in the western developed world, not just in the UK. Since the early 1970s and the recognition of the finiteness of resources and the infiniteness of demand, the position of professionals as the final allocators of resources has been under threat. Some have responded by joining the ranks of managers and seeking to retain power by controlling budgets, others have closed ranks against the new challenge. Terms of employment create differences of perception and styles of working between short-contract managers and tenured medical staff in the NHS. Doctors in hospital or general practice know that once they are established they are likely to be working with the same colleagues for most of their professional life. Compromises and trade-offs are likely to be the hallmark of their relationships (Aaron and Schwartz 1984). Managers who individually move on in their careers, although reputation is important, expect to be able to address problems and to bring about change with less regard for personalities or long-term peer group relationships. In social work, nursing and the paramedical professions, management is generally exercised by professionally qualified colleagues, but often these are seen to be remote from direct client/patient contact.

Public versus private funding

The tension here goes deep into political ideology. The principle of the public provision of health and welfare was enshrined in the establishment of the NHS and in the setting up of the local authority welfare, child care and, later, social service departments. Statutory recognition of the community's responsibility for its needy members goes back to the Elizabethan Poor Law. The rise of the new Right in the last quarter of the 20th century has questioned this principle, and the arguments have been fuelled by concern over rising costs. In the final analysis, the question is whether there is any collective responsibility for individuals or not. In a modified form the question is posed whether services should be privately funded but publicly delivered, or alternatively whether they should be publicly funded but privately delivered. The raising of these questions has sharpened debates about the use of resources, and accountability, and the provisions in the NHS and Community Care Act of 1990 put them to the test.

The emphasis on the market as a guiding principle of the organisation of health and welfare assumes that competition will determine the most effective allocation of funds and resources. Cooperation is not compatible with competition between people and agencies striving to win and survive in a pure deregulated market, because co-operation implies trust and a willingness to share information and resources.

Integration versus separation

The tension here is between what is held in common and can be shared and what needs to be specific and separate. A common task for health and welfare may be perceived, but carried out through a necessary or historical division of labour. The local authority and NHS reorganisations of the early 1970s reflected a strong move to integration: although in England and Wales it stopped short of integrating health and welfare services, it showed itself in the combining of social work at professional, educational and service delivery levels, in the integration of the different branches of nursing under one professional council and in the bringing together of hospital and community medicine in the 1974 NHS reorganisation.

In 1976 the Royal Commission on the National Health Service again considered the possibility of integrating health and local authority services and decided against recommending it. 'The evidence... tended to divide according to the interest of the organisation concerned... it was obvious no radical solution would command general support... but changes are not necessary at present simply to achieve better collaboration between the NHS and local authorities' (DHSS 1979a).

In the UK there has been one significant exception. In Northern Ireland single management structures under four ministerially appointed Health and Social Services Boards set up in 1973 are responsible for both Health and Social Services. Funding for both is central, and competition for resources is therefore internal.

Apart from this exception, the integration of Health and Social Services in organisational, operational and funding terms has not so far been found to be politically or practically feasible.

The tension between integration and separation is seen not only in organisations and agencies but also in the organisation of skills and knowledge. Professions have sought to protect their autonomy and to establish recognised specialities. The recognition that these alone are often incapable of addressing complex personal and social situations has led either to attempts to co-ordinate the work of different specialities, or to the search for generic training based on common core skills and knowledge. The tension between specialist and generic affects all attempts at interprofessional work.

The organisation of health and welfare services and the search for social justice and efficiency

Changes in organisation, structures and management

Until the 1970s both Health and Social Services continued with the organisational patterns which had been set after the Second World War. The National Health Service was tripartite, with separate structures for general practice, hospital and community services independent of each other.

The local authority welfare services had continued to develop in a piecemeal fashion, with the welfare and mental welfare officers carrying out functions descended from the Poor Law, and, in 1948, the new children's departments staffed by an emerging professional group of child care officers.

In both health and welfare in the 1960s concern grew about the costs of duplication and the failure of fragmented services to meet people's needs. Economic fears combined with political pressure and changing management philosophies to produce a search for equity and efficiency through reorganisation. Social Services was the first to move to a more integrated organisation in 1970 after the Seebohm Report of 1968 recommended a generic service with a 'one door' policy. The NHS followed in 1974. The idea which influenced the reorganisations not only of the NHS and the welfare services but also of local authorities generally was that of corporate rationalism, which sought through planning, management and budgeting to meet needs in the public sector both equitably and efficiently. The structures set up were bureaucratic, stratified and hierarchical and the mechanisms used were central accountability, the separation of strategic from operational planning and financial control through, in the case of the NHS, cash limits.

The reforms were essentially structural and managerial, not philosophical, and demand-led health and welfare services were still unquestioned. However, economic pressures grew and by 1981 the then Secretary of State for Social Services wrote: 'New health authorities and their partners in local government will face a common challenge in providing the best possible services *within the limits of available resources* [my italics]' (DHSS 1981a). The shift from a demand-led service to a supply-controlled one had begun.

In the 1980s the NHS underwent a rapid succession of organisational and managerial changes; in the search for efficiency management by consensus became discredited. General managers were appointed to take control and the emphasis was on the control of inputs, the pursuit of quantifiable measures of efficiency and clear lines of responsibility and accountability. Until the 1970s the meeting of need was acknowledged as a legitimate organisational pursuit; by the 1980s the containment of cost had become predominant. The reduction of public expenditure, rather than the pursuit of equity, became the guiding principle. The local authority social service departments escaped the central reorganisations imposed by government, but the strain of increasingly capped resources in the face of rising demand changed the patterns of service set in 1970 and in 1974. Genericism in service delivery, practice and social work education began to be questioned in the light of public and media demands for adequate responses to child abuse and psychiatric care. There was a growing but initially implicit return to specialist knowledge and skills, later formalised in a retreat from generic teams to specialist teams, with a managerial and resource preference given to child and family work, and specialist qualifications granted for some work in mental illness.

Years of argument around nursing qualifications resulted finally in agreed policies for change (United Kingdom Capital Council 1986) and nursing schools entered into partnerships with institutions of higher education for the teaching and validation of courses. Similar arrangements were pioneered for physiotherapy, speech therapy and occupational therapy. The pressures underlying these changes included the desire for greater recognition as professions to be reckoned with and the need to be equipped to survive in the developing managerial culture.

The 1990 NHS and Community Care Act addressed the organisation and management of the services in a radical fashion. It introduced the idea of the market as a guiding principle for the distribution of resources. Individuals, through the agency of general practitioners and care managers holding budgets, were to have purchasing power. Needs were to determine which services developed. Contracts were to be the means of relating within internal markets. The purchaser, with the responsibility of determining the needs of populations, communities and individuals, had to contract with a range of providers, including the private and voluntary sectors.

Despite political claims that the NHS and the welfare state are not under attack, the original ideals of equity and the pursuit of social justice have faded behind the pursuit of economic efficiency and the concept of the consumer within a market as its tool. The turmoil and changes in the organisation, funding, management and service delivery of health and welfare have been the background to any attempts to pursue interprofessional and interagency collaboration.

Interagency and interprofessional collaboration as a response to the political failure to integrate health and welfare

Once it had been accepted as politically difficult, if not impossible, to combine health and social services structurally, the problem of overcoming this separation had to be faced.

In 1972 Sir Keith Joseph, then Secretary of State for Social Services, wrote: '[we are required] to concentrate instead on ensuring that the two parallel authorities – one local, one health – with their separate statutory responsibilities shall work together in partnership for the Health and Social Care of the population' (Alsopp 1984).

Government documents acknowledged: 'Health and Social needs interact, therefore services interrelate' (DHSS 1973). In 1979 *Patients First* (DHSS 1979a) recognised again that the transfer of the NHS to local government, or Social Services to the NHS, or Family Practitioner Committees to District Health Authorities 'would not command general support'. The Royal Commission on the NHS in 1979 argued that effective collaboration was possible without structural merging (DHSS 1979a). In 1985 the House of Commons Second Report from the Social Services Committee on Community Care with reference to adult mental illness and mental handicap spelled out most specifically, 'Some means of eventually bringing the services together is desirable which would not destroy the present integration of Social Services with the local authority services, nor diminish the priority given by either the NHS or the local authorities to mandatory services' (House of Commons 1985). Public Policy documents [see Appendix A] make clear the tensions and ambivalence between integration and separation and that collaboration as a public policy is intended to overcome the disadvantages of separation without facing the difficulties of integration. A clear message emerges. Collaboration is about *bridging the gap*. Collaboration in government philosophy has generally been accepted as self-evidently *'a good thing'*, which will lead to desirable goals such as patient satisfaction and the economic use of resources.

From an examination of the briefs and forewords of many of the government documents set out in Appendix A it is evident that there never has been a coherent philosophy of collaboration, nor any hard evidence quoted for most of the assumptions made. However, three main themes emerge; *meeting needs comprehensively; the pursuit of economies, efficiency and effectiveness; and gain to the professions.*

Meeting needs comprehensively as a purpose of collaboration comes through strongly in many of the government policy documents, from the 1971 *Better Services for the Mentally Handicapped* (DHSS 1971), through the 1976 Court Report and its pursuit of integrated services for children, to the comprehensive care advocated by the 1986 Cumberlege Report. Underlying the extolling of comprehensive services is the recognition of need, both individual and community. The Court Report 1976 speaks of client benefit, the Jay Report 1979 of meeting needs. In 1982 the DHSS Report on NHS restructuring calls for services responsive to needs and in 1984 the DHSS Report on collaboration between family practitioner committees and district health authorities puts collaboration forward as a means of serving the interests of the community. A Government Paper on collaboration between the NHS, local government and voluntary organisations (DHSS 1986c) spelled out most fully that close co-ordination of services is necessary so that 'each person's individual needs may be effectively and economically met' The 1990 NHS and Community Care Act refers to assessment of needs by the local authority and the associated providers of services and expects there to be a mutual exchange of information if the assessment and provision involves different agencies.

The second theme is *economies, efficiency and effectiveness.* The words 'efficient' and 'effective' appear again and again in all the documents alongside the idea of rationalisation and of overcoming duplication which is assumed to be wasteful and therefore inefficient. None of these words are defined, their meanings seem to be taken for granted, as does collaboration as a means of achieving them. 'Effective, efficient use of resources' (DHSS 1973), 'Effective development of resources' (DHSS 1976), 'Cost effective' appears in 1982 (DHSS 1982) and in 1984 in setting out collaboration between FPCs and DHAs, where the 'rationalisation of services and resources' is also seen as a purpose to release resources for development (DHSS 1984). *'Progress in Partnership'* in 1986 spoke of 'the right mix of services', 'avoiding gaps and duplication' and 'improving the use of resources'(Local Authorities and National Association of Health Authorities 1986). 'The effective and economic meeting of needs' appears in the 1986 document on collaboration (DHSS 1986).

Successive governments have promoted a policy of developing community based services 'so that people are kept out of hospital and other institutions, and supported within the community'. (DHSS 1976). This policy was directed particularly at the 'Cinderella services', which were later identified as priority groups and services, priority in strategic terms but not in finance. In 1981 *Care in Action* (DHSS 1981) defined four priority groups of people, the elderly, the mentally ill and the mentally and physically handicapped. Collaboration in the community was seen as an essential part of a strategy for the care of these large groups of people, for whose needs the resources were historically underfunded. Some of this stress on community services stemmed from a developing emphasis on a philosophy of normalisation as an ideal for meeting the needs of mentally ill and mentally impaired people, as opposed to institutionalisation, but it also developed for reasons of cost and a so far unsubstantiated belief that community services are cheaper than hospital services. Community care developed and expanded in the 1980s across a range of health and welfare agencies, public and private, only to be criticised in the Audit Commission's Report of 1986 for wastefulness and confusion. The Griffiths Report of 1988 recommended that local authorities become the lead agencies, but it was not until 1993 that the provisions of the 1990 Act were implemented and community care was based on the same principles of purchaser/provider splits. The assumption that a variety of agencies were to be involved in the efficient meeting of individual and community needs was implicit.

The third theme in government policy documents is *gain to the professions.* The appeal to the interests of the professions emerges in the expectation that the agencies and professionals involved will experience a mutuality which will promote and be enhanced by collaboration. This encompasses mutual goals, needs and concerns (DHSS 1973), through a common challenge and the benefit of sharing resources (DHSS 1981b) to a direct appeal to professional self-interest from Cumberlege Report (1986) which argued that a fuller use of nurses' skills will make both the doctors' and the nurses' jobs more satisfying.

Collaboration in public policy has not therefore been seen as desirable in its own right. It has emerged as a means to a variety of ends: to meeting the health and welfare needs of communities or individuals; as a necessary component of the policy of Community Care; as an implicit means of promoting the teamwork envisaged in Primary Health Care or Neighbourhood Nursing, or as a way of avoiding inefficient and uneconomic duplication of services.

Tools for collaboration

The means of promoting collaboration have gradually built up in successive public policy documents [Appendix A], and tools and mechanisms have become more detailed as public policy has progressed. In 1971 (Cmnd. 4683, DHSS 1971) it was enough to rest on exhortation to good practice and appeal to good will. By 1986 papers were advocating formal agreements (Cumberlege Report 1986) and requiring Annual Reports to the Minister (DHSS 1986c). By 1990 Community Care as a formal means of collaboration was recognised statutorily, but the responsibility for implementing it was placed on one agency, the local authority, not on all possible parties. The top-down approach of public policy rests on statute, requiring the setting up of formal structures, the allocation of funding, the detailing of procedures. Initially this was at a very general level of exhortation from central government, then the 1973 NHS White Paper suggested statutory guidelines, saying: 'Collaboration is too important to be left [only] to good practice'(NHS Reorganisation Act 1973). The 1977 NHS Act laid a statutory duty to co-operate on health and local authorities. In the foreword to *Care in Action* (DHSS 1981a), the Minister addressed himself to members both of district health authorities and local authority Social Service Committees: 'I want to see as close a collaboration as possible'.

The 1973 NHS Act addressed itself specifically to the practices and procedures of collaboration. It laid out four categories of collaboration, which were sharing of services, co-ordination of service delivery, joint planning and joint prevention. The greatest emphasis was on joint planning for the development of community services for the priority care groups. The 1973 Act emphasised planning and provision of services, the development of effective links and the co-ordination of the allocation of resources and sharing facilities. The stress on building formal and informal links for officers and members was repeated in 1984 and 1986 (DHSS 1984 and 1986c), and the need for communication, the sharing of information and the assurance of full information was set out in 1979 (DHSS 1979a), 1984 (DHSS) and 1985 (House of Commons), and in 1990. The importance of agreeing procedures, identifying 'the purpose, form and resource implications' (DHSS 1979a) and those priority groups and services (DHSS 1981a) involved were recognised as first steps in realisable collaboration, while 'realism' itself as a necessary principle was raised in 1985 (House of Commons). Another principle, 'simplicity', was named in 1982 (DHSS).

The first collaborative structures of the reorganised National Health Service in 1974 were Joint Consultative Committees of members of Area Health Authorities and Local Authority Social Service Committees. At this time the conterminosity or overlapping of geographical boundaries was considered important to ensure identical spheres of responsibility and influence. This principle was reduced in importance in the 1979 *Patients First* (DHSS 1979b), which gave priority to internal NHS organisational demands. Joint Consultative

Committees were strengthened in 1976 with the setting up of Joint Care Planning Teams which were intended to be concerned with strategic planning rather than with detailed practice. Joint Finance, that is central money transferred from health authorities for joint purposes with local authorities serving their patients, was made available. In 1986 Joint Consultative Committees were strengthened in importance *vis-à-vis* their parent authorities in that their work was subject to review and assessment, including an Annual Report to the Minister.

Structures and financial mechanisms for collaboration in Community Care were judged as inadequate in the Griffiths Report (1988). Clarity on objectives, priorities and standards, reviewing local plans against national objectives, and arranging individual packages of care were seen as necessary. One agency to take a lead role was seen as essential to produce coherence and take account of real impediments to collaboration.

That interagency or interprofessional collaboration is difficult is never spelled out in public policy documents, but is implicitly recognised in the emphasis on attitudes. In 1979 the Royal Commission (DHSS 1979a) suggested that success depends on the attitude (not defined) of the parties, and later *Patients First* (DHSS 1976b) appealed to determination and the will to work together. Joint planning, the House of Commons Committee commented in 1985, 'depends on a sense that those involved are basically in the same business' (House of Commons 1985). No acknowledgement that being in the same business can as easily lead to conflict and competition as to co-operation.

Power as a necessary tool in collaboration was recognised in the recommendation of the Royal Commission in 1979 that officers of sufficient seniority within their own authorities should engage in joint planning, so that action can be effective. In 1984 it was recommended not only that officers should be senior, but that they should also be at appropriate levels in each organisation to take decisions, and to have control over finance and policy. Considering family practitioner committees as partners in joint planning in 1984 and 1986 pointed to an understanding that agencies needed sufficient autonomy to be taken seriously by the others, 'to claim a place as of right at the planning table'.

Following the 1990 Act, with its division between purchasers and providers, the Audit Commission 1992 recommended horizontal partnerships across agency and organisational boundaries between purchasers on the one hand, possibly setting up Joint Commissioning, and service providers on the other. Such partnerships have role and function in common.

Within public policy, skills, knowledge and training for collaboration has received the least attention. In 1973 (DHSS) it was acknowledged that it would be necessary to foster understanding of the need for co-operation, and in 1979 the Jay Report commended joint training for staff working with mentally impaired people, a recommendation subsequently acted upon by the Nursing and Social Work training councils. Appropriate training in the importance of collaboration was advocated by the Royal Commission in 1979 and shared training was proposed in 1979 (DHSS 1979a) and by the NHS Training Authority in 1986 (DHSS 1086a). Not until the *Progress in Partnership* Report (Local Authorities Association and National Association of Health Authorities) in 1986 was it even suggested that collaboration itself might require not only structures, finance and appropriate attitudes but also skills, and even then it is one brief recommendation among several that there should be 'training in joint planning and working at all levels'. Working together as a means of achieving collaboration at service delivery level has been seen as a strategy since the 1976 Court Report's proposal for multi-disciplinary teams for child health, as though multi-disciplinary working would of itself motivate agencies and professionals to learn about each other and develop skills in collaboration. This expectation, that working together would promote working together, was most explicitly spelt out in *Progress in Partnership,* which proposed an interactive approach to collaboration, rather than one dictated from above.

Knowing how to collaborate as well as knowing about collaboration emerged in 1986 in the Green Paper on primary health care (DHSS 1986d) and the Cumberlege Report on neighbourhood nursing. Both identified the need for skills and encouraged the effective use of skills and knowledge in working together as part of developing the full potential of professionals. The NHS Training Authority recognised that training was necessary to cross professional boundaries, and the 'Health Pick Up' scheme proposed working with others as part of its educational programme.

Since 1990, the Department of Health has exhorted funding bodies to promote and commission multi-disciplinary and shared learning to meet present and future employment needs. At the same time, through the emphasis on vocational training and qualification, there has been the search for core skills. The suspicion is abroad that the goal might be a generic therapist who would embody collaboration. Another untested device.

The purpose and possible means of collaboration are set out in public policy, but there is no one clear expression of a philosophy of collaboration. The policy documents reflect a confusion of conflicting goals and values to which collaboration between health and welfare is supposed to contribute. This confusion demonstrates how difficult it is to reach common ground even at a general level. The documents, set out at different times but within a relatively short time, span such opposing values in health and welfare as the comprehensive response to individual needs and the pursuit of economy and efficiency; a service demand-led by needs or one controlled by supply-limited resources; a service responsive to local community needs or one with central government strategies governing the allocation of finance; services dominated by professionals, or by managers;

political consensus or markets and competition; publicly accountable or private provision.

There are, however, implicit understandings in successive documents which illuminate what underlies the common sense idea of collaboration as a 'good thing'. At the most general level, there is a recognition that 'health services cannot be operated in isolation [from]... a range of closely related services which are the responsibility of Local Government' (DHSS 1973), which appears again in the 1981 (DHSS 1981a) 'health and social services are part of the broad spectrum of care'. Underlying these statements of the self-evident, there is an implicit model of health and welfare which is more comprehensive than a model of illness. But the appeal to an underlying holistic model makes assumptions which are difficult to follow for agencies and professions working on a base of specialist responsibilities and tasks. The lack of an explicit basis for the requirement of collaboration means that the difficulties tend to be put down to the failure of organisation, or awkward attitudes, or the lack of skills, and the consequent call for education and training does nothing to explain or address the sources of the difficulties. Calls for realism and simplicity as guiding principles continue to beg the question.

Of all the documents concerned with collaboration, only one, the 1984 *Report of the Joint Working Group on Collaboration between Family Practitioner Committees and District Health Authorities* (DHSS 1984), explicitly attempted to identify the Principles of Collaboration. It recommended a policy of minimum, practicable, variable change, simple structures and tried and proved management and planning processes, recommendations aimed no doubt at making the Report's proposals as acceptable as possible to a professional group traditionally suspicious of anything resembling bureaucracy, but it goes on to set out basic precepts, starting with mutual understanding and respect for each other's role and responsibility; identification of areas of common interest and concern; the establishment and pursuit of common goals, policies and programmes. For nearly 25 years a succession of policy documents on health and welfare have recognised the place for collaboration as relevant in the meeting of need, but collaboration itself has not been spelt out, nor is it mandatory (neither is it in legislation to do with children). Recommendations hoping to make it possible have included exhortation and expectation, even addressing attitude; the setting up of shared committees and teams for planning, communication and service delivery; joint finance and realistic allocation of resources; the identification of priority groups of people spanning health and welfare boundaries; formal programmes of community care and responsibility for them allocated to one lead agency; the need for similar status, power and autonomy; the place of training in skills and knowledge and the need to experience working together.

The responses to the 'top-down' encouragement of public policy have, at local levels, been very varied. Professional staff have been appointed to liaise across organisational boundaries. Project groups around social issues such as drug abuse or care of elderly people have involved joint funding and multi-disciplinary teams. Alliances have been formed with the voluntary sector and housing associations to serve mentally ill people. Health promotion programmes have provided a focus for teamwork. Health visitors and counsellors are attached to group general practices. Community care packages for elderly people include service from the private sector.

Research

There has been no extensive research to give a comprehensive account of the range of collaborative enterprise which has developed since 1973. Reports of activities have been published in many different areas – research documents, papers to policy committees, and articles in professional journals. The very nature of the political, organisational, professional and educational environment which creates the need for collaboration also makes it difficult to get a coherent picture.

Community care has been the object of study for much of the formal research, which attempts to be more rigorous than the many descriptive accounts appearing in journals. Twenty-eight projects were studied by the Personal Social Services Research Unit at the University of Kent (Renshaw *et al.* 1988). Bristol University's School of Advanced Urban Studies evaluated six community care projects (Smith 1993). Action researchers into collaboration between five different agencies involved in the care of elderly, mentally frail people wrote up a project from inside (Dartington 1986) and similarly skills were explored in community care programmes (Beresford and Trevillion 1995). Research such as this seeks to analyse issues which are significant in the success or difficulties of collaborative work. These issues are as varied as the conditions set out in the policy documents and include the need for allocated finance, clarity about accountability, the need for mutual trust, agreement on leadership and resources of authority, training in skills and knowledge, continuity of relationships and shared location and adequate time.

A fruitful source of reflection on collaboration has come from studies of social work in health care, both in this country and in the USA. Most of this literature has been written by social workers seeking to learn from the difficulties they experience in making their contribution in fields dominated by the medical profession. As early as 1965 a medical social worker published the first book in this country (Collins 1965); more recently issues such as the advantages of social workers being placed in hospitals or on general practitioner attachments, the management of anxiety, rivalry with nursing, professional ideologies and tribalism, multi-disciplinary assessment, small group processes, team work, were considered in two publications with a similar title, *Social Work and/in Health Care* (Taylor and Ford 1989; Davidson and Clark 1990). The social work centenary public lecture (Platt 1995) addresses the changing systems of health and community care and argues for commissioners to take a more holistic approach to their task if people's needs are to be fully met.

If the 'top-down' approach to collaboration draws on public policy, the 'bottom-up' approach relies on research, description and reflection. Together they begin to address common themes which highlight the difficulties of collaboration and suggest some of the conditions for success. But apart from the fact that broadly the same phenomenon is being addressed, there is little coherence.

Conclusion

However health and welfare services are organised the consequent limitations on the planning and delivery of care are bound to cut across the range of physical, emotional and social needs experienced by individuals and communities. An organisation large enough to meet all these needs would fall apart under the strain of internal co-ordination. An organisation small enough to be comprehensible to individuals and local communities is unlikely to be able to contain on its own a sufficient range of expertise and resources to meet the complexity of needs.

The philosophy of collaboration as it threads through the public policies implicitly weaves together assumptions of an encompassing model of health, comprehensive and integrated care, the meeting of individual and community needs, and mutual interest for agencies and professionals.

But little of this is made explicit, and the common assumption seems to be that the separation of health and local authority services gives rise to wasteful duplication, costly gaps and undeveloped potential, all of which apparently-undesirable results collaboration is intended to overcome. The question still to be answered is, does it? And further, could it be that the costs of collaboration might outweigh the supposed costs of not collaborating?

If collaboration between health and local authorities and between the associated professions is to develop effectively when it is necessary, research needs to identify collaborative work and evaluate it against well-founded criteria. Exhortation, funding, organisation and skills have emerged piecemeal in public policies as necessary conditions for interagency and interprofessional collaboration.

Most of what is written up tends to be either an account of success or a rehearsal of difficulties. Collaboration itself has not been much examined either as a concept or as a practice. Unless this is done, agencies and professionals trying to work together are often reinventing the wheel, or, worse, are pursuing a myth which by its existence is preventing the search for other ways of meeting needs effectively, efficiently and comprehensively.

CHAPTER TWO

Why Collaboration in Health and Welfare
Its Place in Ideology, Models of Care and Social Theory

To achieve effective collaboration the word itself must be removed from political rhetoric and the realm of common sense where it is too often found. If this can be done, then the case for collaboration need be made only when it is likely to be effective, claims for resources can be justified, practitioners can be held accountable, and skills and knowledge can be explicit, taught and transferable.

Activities are always based on assumptions about purpose and values and necessary conditions, whether such assumptions are made explicit or not. In collaboration between health and welfare, assumptions are made about the nature of health, about the role of collaboration in providing care, and about how people work together. If these assumptions can be explored, then the function and methods of collaboration may become clearer.

This chapter, therefore, argues that considering ideologies of health and models of care, and exploring some social theories which explain how and why people work together, may illuminate some of the largely hidden assumptions. Some basic ideas will be identified to point toward a fuller understanding of the necessary conditions for collaboration.

Practice and theory

The search for a framework of concepts relevant to a theory and practice of collaboration explores some theories and practices current in the delivery of health and social care since the middle years of the 20th century. Knowledge is both *deductive*, that is, drawn from theory, and *inductive*, that is, drawn from experience.

Professional practice draws both on theory, usually learnt mostly on pre-qualifying courses and sometimes continued with post-qualifying study, and on practice, not necessarily only that of the individual but of the professional group, insofar as it is written up or codified and seen to be of a sufficiently general nature. In social work teaching, this intermediate knowledge was known as 'practice wisdom'. Knowledge based on theory and knowledge based on practice feed each other and interact to produce knowledge which is applicable and found to be useful. Such an interaction is part of all human service professions and practitioners base their work on assumptions drawn from it. Practice very often allows little time for reflection, so such assumptions usually become implicit rather than explicit, and at risk of being unexamined. If such assumptions can be examined and evaluated and their sources made clear, whether in theory or in practice, then a claim for resources may be argued and accounted for more knowledgeably by the practitioners, managers and policy-makers.

The appeal to collaboration has largely rested on assumptions that it is 'a good thing' and these assumptions have been little explored. Collaborative activities have been much described. The associated difficulties have been much discussed. Teaching for collaborative skills has on the whole been driven by a recognition of the difficulties and the consequent desire to equip practitioners to get round them, for example, difficulties in communication, therefore teach people communication skills; mutual incomprehension, therefore teach professionals about each other. As a consequence collaboration is being understood mostly inductively; that is, from practice. So far, a theory of collaboration, for collaboration in practice, is very undeveloped. Without such a theory, practice struggles to make sense of itself and is hampered by the lack of any dialogue with a coherent framework of ideas leading to transferable knowledge and skills.

The social theories explored in the search for relevant concepts are among those which attempt to understand the interaction between individuals and groups as they live and work together, experiencing and meeting needs in a world of finite resources. Collaboration implies an interaction between at least two parties. The search for a conceptual framework therefore includes a consideration of some general social theory relating to interaction, General Systems Theory, Social Exchange Theory and Co-operation Theory.

To elicit a useful understanding of practice it is necessary to consider some of the philosophies and ideologies which colour people's assumptions about health and welfare. These philosophies and ideologies underlie particular models of health and welfare services, which determine models of intervention, the range of skills and methods and the form of organisation. As collaboration takes place within a social context, it becomes necessary to refer to ideologies which colour social organisation, such as capitalism and the market allocation of resources, socialism and state intervention, and humanist and ecological perspectives. These ideologies inform models of health and welfare which determine the mode and focus of interventions. Concepts affecting collaboration are therefore to be sought in models of health and welfare, the range of interventions, and the organisation and management of resources such as knowledge, skills, time and material goods.

The pursuit of health

People throughout history and in all societies have tried to find an explanation for the experience of disease and an understanding of health, physical, mental and social, as both a state and a goal. Such explanations and understandings are not very often spelt out by practitioners and policy-makers, but colour their implicit assumptions affecting their values and choices. Health is individually or socially defined and individually and socially determined. It is recognised at individual and social levels which are inextricably linked because people's lives are lived both individually and in communities.

At an individual level the understanding of health in developed western societies has been predominantly categorised by biological and medical science, and the medical model of intervention is primarily intended to cure, to restore or maintain, a person's normal functioning. Within this model of intervention, collaboration between different agents of intervention may be necessary either because the needs change over time and require different specialist contributions, or because the situation is too complex for any one practitioner acting alone.

At a community level the understanding of health is informed by both biological, environmental and social knowledge, and intervention is intended to prevent disease or disability, to control the spread or rise of disease states within a population, and to promote health by creating the conditions which support it. Collaboration within this model is necessary because the situations being addressed are likely to be recognised as multi-factorial, involving a wide range of players.

There are other perspectives. Political and philosophical critics have attacked the use powerful professional and economic interests have made of the prevailing models of health and intervention which serve, it is argued, to maintain their power, and have proposed alternative understandings which would lead to different responses. Illich (1975) defines the concept of health as a life task, of adaptation to problems of living. He warns against the medicalisation of health, that is, allowing health to be defined only in medical terms and so handing power over it to the medical profession, and argues that the health of the individual and the health of the society in which she/he lives are one and the same. Dubos (1979) suggests that health is an ecological concept related to the social environment, in which people continually seek change and challenge, 'Earth has never been a Garden of Eden, but a Valley of Decision where resilience is essential to survival'. The Judaeo-Christian religious understanding of health as Wholeness or Salvation, both individual and corporate, warns against seeing the pursuit of health as a problem to be solved, rather as a means to learning and growth: 'Health is... a value and a vision' (Jenkins 1990) to be pursued as an unfinished task, and to be a measure of the quality of life. The emergence of the emphasis in some parts of health and welfare provision on the centrality of the user/patient/client in the planning and delivery of service chimes in with the perceptions of these critics.

Such philosophical and religious understandings have informed the thinking of the World Health Organisation which has transformed them into goals and principles and then into programmes. The Declaration of Alma Ata, an international conference on primary health care held in 1978, restated the familiar definition of health as 'a state of complete physical, mental and social well-being' (WHO 1978) and added that it 'is a fundamental human right,... the attainment of the highest possible level of health is a most important worldwide social goal whose realisation requires the action of many other social and economic sectors in addition to the health sector'. The strategies which followed are the pursuit of care in and by the community, the promotion of the concept of primary health care understood not only in UK terms but also in particular ways related to the needs of underdeveloped countries, and the strategy of the 'healthy city' dependent on the concept of 'intersectoral collaboration'. In the Copenhagen Declaration the European WHO Regional Office translated the Alma Ata Declaration into 38 specific targets to be attained by the year 2000. The translation of principles and targets into policies and practice becomes the task of societies and governments. It is at this level of intervention that there ceases to be agreement on what is self-evidently desirable. The delivery of health and social care enters the domain of *realpolitik* and is subject to all the diverse views of a sophisticated and complex society. Some of these diverse means may be seen in the conflict between integration and differentiation, centralisation and localisation, professional and managerial dominance, competition and co-ordination, allocation by need and allocation by resources, and specialism and generalism. In the pursuit of health through social and economic policies, and the political contexts which affect them, such conflicting concepts become attached to different ideologies. The measures of costs and outputs, the allocation and sources of resources and the organisation and accountability of services are coloured by political values and lead to prevailing modes of financing, managing and delivering services.

Under a government dominated by capitalist assumptions, health is seen as a commodity, bestowed by some members of society upon others, and competed for as are other commodities. It is managed and determined by experts, and people become consumers or customers, who challenge the experts for sufficient information to make choices. Because it is perceived as a commodity, it becomes unevenly spread throughout society and the responsibility for possessing it is laid upon the individual. The capitalist emphasis on the market supply of goods and labour, and the perception of the state as non-interventionist, leaves the attainment and maintenance of health at the mercy of economic values, supported by the appeal to the virtues of freedom and choice for the individual who takes personal responsibility for his/her lifestyle and its consequences.

The Marxist critique claims that the internal logic of capitalism with its priorities and values explains the underdevelopment of health in a society dedicated to the reproduction of capital and the political and social control of surplus population. The state cannot be disinterested but works to sustain the power of its dominant groups.

Under a government influenced by socialist assumptions, health is perceived as a right of citizenship, to be pursued by social action such as redistributive justice. This involves the state in the collective provision of goods and labour, and measures of social engineering which acquire their own momentum and give rise to bewilderment among the managers and professionals when the people resist their well-meaning programmes, for example, the failure to attain 100 per cent immunisation. The dilemma is that health and welfare services under such a system are entirely demand-led and have to respond to diseases and social problems over whose causes they have no control. The diseases or problems may be caused by the behaviour of individuals or by the social, economic or physical conditions in society, but however they are caused those who determine the cause incur no economic cost and can benefit, directly if not indirectly, from free treatment. The cost of pursuing even such desirable social goals as health through collectivist means may involve an unacceptable or unmanageable degree of control over individual choices, whilst the pursuit of health as a commodity belonging to individuals results in an abdication of social responsibility for the environment within which people live. Conflict is therefore endemic in the provision of health and welfare and any current consensus is always unstable.

Understanding what affects the delivery of health and social care involves recognising and acknowledging the existence of powerful groupings which have their own interests to pursue and maintain. Policies such as community care, or primary health care or collaboration, will be judged in terms of the associated losses or gains for such groups, whether they are professionals, or managers, or organised workers, or consumers. In this interplay of powerful interests governments use or are used by them, and the pursuit of policies will not be disinterested. For example, the promotion of WHO programmes stressing community action and community care was vigorously harnessed by faculties of community medicine, who lost a great deal of influence when the functions and role of the medical officers of health were transferred from the local authority to the hospital-dominated health authorities in 1974. The

Faculty of Community Medicine (1985) published a Charter for Action which stressed promotion and prevention and argued for a reorientation of health care systems 'so that they not only respond to medical problems but are sensitive to social and psychological needs'.

The competition to become the lead agency in community care was between health authorities whose dominant profession was doctors, and local authorities through the social services. Primary health care led by general practitioners is in competition with the secondary health care sectors for finance and the allocation of work. Such competition is part of the political scene and is used by governments in pursuit of their goals.

The price paid for a limited understanding, organisation and account of health care, not only in the actual costs of delivery but also in terms of distortion of priorities, is seen in the growing divide between the health of the prosperous and the disease of the poor, both within and between countries. This divide is coming to be recognised not only as morally undesirable, but politically dangerous. It is apparent that either the individual pursuit of health or the collectivist pursuit of health each taken on its own to its ultimate conclusion becomes a meaningless dead end. Health is not a product, but a process of interaction within and between individuals and the societies in which they live. The recognition of health and welfare within society as an interactive, adaptive process without an end becomes the only creative basis for strategies, policies and practices. In this interactive process, by definition, the ability to collaborate is essential.

Models of health and disease

In European society both the early Christian church's dualism between the sinful body and the good soul, and the 18th-century development of scientific rationalism, led to Descarte's understanding of the body as a self-contained mechanical system which could be observed, described and treated. The mind was separate. It had no spatial properties, was accessible only through intro-spection and therefore was thought not to be amenable to scientific study and knowledge. The body became understood as the locus for disease, to be treated mechanistically within a model of medicine which included a disease label, a passive patient and a medical expert. By the early 20th century it was thought disease had a specific cause, either an invasion, a lesion or a stress, which could be identified and treated and cured through the application of knowledge drawn from the natural sciences and applied by scientifically educated practi-tioners. This model of illness is essentially bio-medical, individualistic, clinical, reductionist and episodic. Its influence is still strong in high-technology acute medicine, and in the social prestige and power conferred on its practitioners.

Alongside the growth of this model, under the influence of the development of psychology and its psychoanalytic application, there developed in the mid 20th century the bio-psycho-social model of medicine, and with it an extending repertoire of interpersonal skills for doctors especially general practitioners, and nurses. The philosophical base of this approach is humanist rather than scientific. For example, 'The physician's role is very much that of educator and psychotherapist. To know how to induce peace of mind in the patient and enhance his faith in the healing powers of his physician requires psychological knowledge and skills, not merely charisma' (Engel 1977). Such developments have been closely associated with the idea of holistic, that is whole person, medicine, but this medical understanding of 'social' is generally confined to an individual or family, at most small-group, perspective and is equated with 'cultural'.

A similar model of welfare as relating to an individual, a family, or at its widest a neighbourhood community was the basis for the development of social work, particularly as long as it emphasised case work with individuals. With the mid 20th century concern with poverty and the rise of civil rights movements, such an emphasis was criticised as inadequate for effective intervention in the social problems experienced by clients. A wider understanding of 'social' emerged, to include economic and political dimensions. Although therefore work with the psycho-social interaction of individual experience was generally understood by caseworkers as the model of welfare from which they drew their mandate, the economic and political extension of the meaning of social based on a 'predominantly social structural theory of causation yields a different locus and mode of intervention, which is usually at odds with the clinical orientation of medicine' (Huntington 1986). Although this may be recognised by practitioners and managers in practice, they largely feel themselves powerless as professionals, though not perhaps as private citizens, to engage in other than the traditional professional spheres of intervention.

The one field of medicine which has been influential in political and economic fields of activity, especially in the past, has been public health, now incorporated in community medicine and environmental health, the one a health service organisation, the other in local authority and not staffed by doctors.

Historically in the UK, especially in the years from the mid 19th century to the early 20th century, the passing of public health measures reduced the incidence of water and airborne diseases which could be controlled by legislation, public works, immunisation or isolation. The environmental, population-based field of activity for medically trained epidemiologists rests on an ecological and biological model of health, which is strongest when major environmental causes of disease are recognised as the responsibility of the whole society. In the 19th century clean water was the result of a succession of Acts of Parliament and major engineering works and in the mid 20th century clean air was achieved by legislation, that is by public action not individual choice. The control today of the adverse effects, for example, of the proliferation of private transport is much more complex and difficult to achieve. At the same time, the WHO's philosophy of the 'healthy city' (WHO 1978) and the associated intersectoral collaboration has emphasised again the importance of the ecological-biological model of health and its relation to the structures of a society, so that the concept of health and welfare is inextricably linked with the understanding of social not as cultural, but as structural, the concept familiar to social work.

The overlap between the different models of health and welfare ranging from the individual to the group and on to the population demonstrates that each perspective can only be incomplete; each alone cannot explain nor organise an adequate response to physical, mental or social problems or the maintenance and promotion of health and welfare. The ability to combine and to collaborate is essential.

The range of models of practice

The range of models of practice in the delivery of health and welfare services is organised around cure, prevention, promotion, maintenance and care.

Demographic pressures, social and economic changes and medico-technical developments in the second half of the 20th century have affected the evolution of health and social care as politicians, managers, professionals and users struggle with the costs and implications of needs and services. A continuum across the whole range of response to need extends from intensive high-technology care, and moves on through a range of intermittent care in institutional or domiciliary settings with professional and personal services to, at the other end, permanent care for people requiring full maintenance or containment in a residential establishment.

This continuum has implications for different models of intervention. At one end is the traditional bio-medical model of diagnosis and treatment, leading to rehabilitation and sometimes cure. At the other end the response is based on a long-term care model of bio-psycho-social assessment and the co-ordination of a monitored programme or regime for people with permanent physical or mental impairments or degenerative conditions, leading to amelioration, maintenance or containment.

In reality these different models of intervention are rarely discrete. The experience of patients or clients as they progress through episodes where they require resources from professional, formal networks may begin with a crisis requiring intensive high technology medicine, followed by a period of hospital care followed by supervision from a combination of hospital-based and primary health care based staff, and ending with minimum support in the community. Needs might, on the other hand, slowly manifest themselves with a slow decline of faculties requiring more and more support from informal and then formal networks of professional staff, until perhaps it becomes necessary to move into residential care staffed by a mixture of qualified and support staff.

The policy of community care is based on the model of needs assessment leading to the management of packages of care drawing on a kaleidoscope of formal and informal services within domestic settings. Although the local authority is named as the lead responsible agency, the contribution of a wide range of other health, welfare, statutory and voluntary agencies is expected. The philosophy behind community care is based on that of normalisation, which originated in the attempt to remove stigma from mentally ill and learning impaired people contained in large institutions. The idea of normalisation has developed into the philosophy that the goal of care is to enable and empower patients or clients so that they become participants in the assessment of their needs and the management of the services. For this they need access to information and access to resources, and the power to choose. The ideal model of community care is therefore a complete contrast to the traditional medical model of the powerful expert and the passive patient.

The implications of the late 20th century changes in needs, in the organisation of services and in the possibilities and philosophies of health and social care are enormous, both in terms of cost and the effective use of resources, and in requiring professions and agencies which hitherto set out clear boundaries between acute and chronic, and health and welfare, to smudge and blur these boundaries and to work across them. The need to work together is challenging to professionals whose claim to expertise rests on knowledge and skills which are perceived to be specialist and exclusive.

Specialisation and the division of labour

The basis of specialisation is the division of labour, the organisation of increasing specialisation within a complex whole. The wider the number of divisions and the deeper the degree of specialism, the greater the need for co-ordination in the service of whole people in the complexity of their needs. The recognition of interdependence may be clear, but it is also associated with differences of power and consequent struggles for demarcation and territorial dominance. The more technically based the specialism, the more secure its claim for pre-eminence within its clearly marked out sphere, but trouble arises when such a specialism, say orthopaedics, makes a claim for its authority to go beyond technical competence into spheres where others claim to exercise knowledge and skills, say physical therapists and social workers working to help a person accept a necessary prosthesis which has negative meanings. Alternatively, where knowledge, skills and roles may overlap, the conflict over occupational territory may actually be more acute and demarcation disputes need even more negotiation (Bywaters 1989).

The division of labour in health and welfare is related to different facets of wholes and exists both within and between professions and agencies. It may be classified in relation to the client or patient's status, say a child or aged person; it can relate to the social problem, for example unemployment or illness, even to a part of the body, as in medical specialities; it may be defined by the skills of the worker, for example, therapist or community worker, or it may relate to the population served. It may be a structural divide, such as that between purchaser and provider.

Division of labour is a response to complexity and diversity, but because of differences in power and social status, it is not static. In search of security, status and power, professions and agencies seek to draw into their exclusive domain new responsibilities and skills, competing with others for dominance. Sometimes the value of the division of labour runs counter to a dominant ideology, such as that of genericism in the development of social work in the 1970s, which led to a disavowal of the need for specialisms within an occupation which was seeking a common base to strengthen its attempt to acquire power and influence social policy. The purity of this ideal was soon compromised by the pressure of the expectations of others, such as the media and doctors, who were not interested in the common base of social work but only in outcomes which were felt to be hampered by the lack of specialist knowledge and skills in, say, child care or mental illness. Speciality was seen to give not only expertise, but also credibility.

This chapter has argued that an understanding, an expectation and an experience of health and welfare are not static but are socially defined and socially determined. Philosophies of health implicitly underlie the public policies which determine the organisation and funding of health and welfare services. Models of care and practice are not absolute but are convenient devices in the organisation of service. In reality there is blurring and overlap, which require co-ordination. A division of labour arises because the growth of knowledge and technical advance leads to the development of specialties which are seen to be rational and purposive, but in meeting the needs of whole persons the more the divisions, the greater the interdependence on each other for the effective delivery of service. Health is therefore a process of interaction for both individuals and populations. Interaction implies interrelationships and interdependence. Complexity and diversity have to be taken into account in responding comprehensively and effectively. A range of responses both rhetorical and practical attempt to make complexity and diversity manageable. The management of diversity requires the professions and agencies involved in health and social care to work together. The totality of people's needs challenges the absurdity of infinite self-contained and self-sufficient divisions of labour: the complexity of society and the historical growth and development of valuable skills and detailed knowledge within professions and organisations challenge the adequacies of genericism. If professions and agencies are required to work together, they need to know what makes it possible; working together implies allocating resources, building structures, managing processes and employing skills. Working together requires knowledge and education not only for responding to patients or clients, but also for relating to collateral members of the service network.

Some social theories relevant to an understanding of collaboration

Some of the social theories which are particularly relevant to the issues identified in the previous section are General Systems Theory, which addresses the concept of 'wholes', Social Exchange Theory, which considers social transactions and questions of costs and benefits, and Co-operation Theory, which attempts to illuminate the limits and opportunities of working together.

General Systems Theory

The biologist Ludwig von Bertalanffy, in his study of living organisms and their ecology, began to be aware of the limits of specialist disciplines in addressing complex social problems. He criticised reductionist explanations, and set out to explain wholes, not in metaphysical terms but as scientifically observable entities with a view to identifying regularities and properties which were valid whatever the size of the object of study (Bertalanffy 1971). Von Bertalanffy and his successors developed the concept of 'system', which could be used across all disciplines from physics and biology to the social and behavioural sciences and whose properties were present in all living phenomena. Wholes are more than the sum of their parts, interactions between entities are purposeful, boundaries between them are permeable and cause and effect are not linear but interdependent. The philosophy underlying Systems Theory is of the unity of nature, governed by the same fundamental laws and principles in all its realms. The consequence of the systems approach for health and welfare practice is to challenge the 'nothing but' view of human beings, a challenge applicable equally to the socio-economic explanation of radical social work, the bio-medical explanation of high-tech medicine, the utilitarian explanation of human relations management and the commercial explanation of social interactions as markets.

One of the crucial characteristics of systems relevant to applied service organisations is the exchange across permeable boundaries between one system and its environment, which is of course another system. This exchange in a social system is of energy in the form of goods, knowledge, work, an exchange which is experienced as an interdependent process of events, 'the news of difference which makes a difference' (Ross and Bilson 1989). The exchange is regulated by feedback and through structures, so that stability and meaning are maintained and adaptability is promoted. Without both maintenance and adaptability there would be in all human and social systems an inevitable decline into disorder and dissolution.

General Systems Theory therefore offers a shift of perception from that bounded by separate parts to an understanding of the processes of interaction which take place within and between whole entities. 'Holistic' is therefore not opposed to 'reductionist'. Such an opposition would make it an impossible and overwhelming goal for separate agencies and professions. Instead, using the concept of system it becomes possible to acknowledge parts as themselves separate systems, but also as relating to others within a greater whole which is more than the sum of the parts because the interdependence and interrelating of the parts themselves are recognised as properties of a whole. This may be either one already existing, like a family with individual members, or a new one, like a purchasing consortium spanning several existing agencies.

The key elements from General Systems Theory relevant to an understanding of collaboration are those of interaction and interdependence, the emphasis on the management of processes, the recognition of equifinality(that is the achievement of the same goals from different possible starting points), the acknowledgement of the role of conflict in the evolution of change, the use of network analysis, and the bringing about of shifts in perception. The main insight is that it is possible to manage complexity and difference through the recognition and use of common properties which apply both to the parts and to a whole, experiences which are shared.

Concepts from General Systems Theory have informed or been specifically used in health and welfare models and practice and have influenced management and policy. In management, the idea of holism underlies the promotion of 'corporate management' as Whittington (1979) points out, but the emphasis on control from the top and administrative efficiency fails to acknowledge other systemic properties such as interaction and adaptation. A very influential use of systems thinking has resulted in the development of the bio-psycho-social model in physical and psychiatric care (Engel 1977) and the growth in the idea of holistic medicine. Associated with this is the idea of equifinality, that is, change in any one part of a system will bring about change in others; this has implications for problem definition and the focus of intervention and research. Clare and Corney (1982) show that the interaction between health and social needs means that change can be achieved by working with either.

In the early 1970s there were attempts to apply concepts from General Systems Theory to social work practice. One of the most influential produced a model for network analysis, or mapping of the relevant field for intervention

(Pincus and Minahan 1973). This model set out a descriptive analysis of four key systems which they called the *change agent system*, composed of those employed to bring about change; the *client system*, those who would benefit from the intervention; the *target system*, those who needed to change, and the *action system*, those who worked together to bring about change. Pincus and Minahan's model also developed a problem-solving process, but did not address skills. The significance of it is the clarity it achieves in identifying the client system, and more importantly for an understanding of collaboration, the highlighting of the relationship between the target system and the action system, and of the need for members of the latter to work together and to accrue sufficient power to lever the target system toward the necessary change.

The elements of General Systems Theory which have been specifically applied in interdisciplinary work in family therapy interventions or behaviour modification programmes include the use of responsive feedback to achieve either balance or a shift in perception which brings about the necessary change for growth and development. The desirable change is not necessarily linear or incremental, but may be in the direction of adaptation and an understanding of the meaning and significance of behaviour within the family. The use in family therapy of the concept of boundary or interface within the family, and between the family and the environment, and the management of the process across boundaries is one which could be transferred to an understanding of collaboration, as could the idea of shifts in perception about the problem focus.

Systems Theory then can contribute key ideas about structures and processes to a framework for understanding collaboration. Such a framework could lead to an analysis of the necessary conditions and an indication of the necessary skills. Systems Theory draws attention to relationships, structures, processes and interdependence. It has been widely and credibly applied in the human service professions, and permeates many now taken-for-granted assumptions.

Social Exchange Theory

Anthropological studies which showed that social exchanges were more than barter but carried meanings beyond the market value for the participants were the sources for the development of Social Exchange Theory in the social sciences, such as social psychology, sociology, anthropology and economics. In social exchanges, it is argued, there is a strong element of reciprocity, a calculation of return. The success of an exchange is dependent on some benefit. The benefit may not be direct or in kind as in barter, but may be some other satisfaction, either immediate or delayed or indeed to some other person or group in the social network. There is some element of self-interest in all instances of social exchange, and the incurring of obligation or indebtedness. Bargaining, negotiation and exchange are a function of interdependence

(Challis *et al.* 1988). The processes of social exchanges involve calculations of costs and benefits, recognition of power differences between the participants, the negotiation of expectations and an understanding of roles and relationships. Clarity about these boundaries of roles and relationships is essential to avoid the muddle and confusion which hamper the success of social exchanges.

In trying to understand collaboration, which has within it greater implications of difference and conflict than has the idea of co-operation, which belongs more in the realm of consensus, the concept of social exchange helps to highlight that something is happening, some things are being exchanged, and conditions for the success of exchange are necessary. The medium of exchange between practitioners, managers and policy-makers in interprofessional and interagency collaboration is all the elements which give their work purpose and meaning, especially resources which include clients or patients, information, services, influence, esteem and power. The demand for or possibility of such exchanges may be very threatening, especially if they are perceived as involving the likelihood of loss of power or control. The loss of resources or threats to domain will be seen as costs of collaboration. There are costs of actually setting up or maintaining collaboration which may not be questioned in times of plenty, but which in times of scarcity will need to be clearly offset by perceived benefits. The benefits usually have to be argued for more strongly, because at the beginning they are still in the future whereas the costs can be more immediately calculated. Trade-offs may be necessary to minimise costs or to make compromises between what is ideal and what is practicable. The benefits from social exchanges can multiply, and provide fruitful conditions for further exchanges. The slow build-up of trust between participants who experience successful exchanges, starting with little incidents involving small risk, will develop into social bonds of mutual commitment. Such commitment makes it possible to take greater risks because of the confident prediction that obligations will be met.

A study of Philip Abrams' classic work *Neighbours* (Bulmer 1986) makes a further conclusion of relevance to the concept of collaboration, and that is the importance of being competent to engage in social exchange. Competence includes not only having sufficient power to engage, but also knowing how to take part. The need for people to be trained and to acquire skills is identified, as is the need for conditions conducive to social exchange to be present, such as time, and appropriate social structures and organisation.

There is clearly a conflict between the need for occupations and professions and agencies through the slow growth of trust to build up joint activities to serve their own interests as well as those of clients, and the need for government and policy-makers to introduce new policies. When community care was proposed, perhaps the recognition of the need for it may be understood as the 'shift of perception' referred to as 'second order change' in General Systems

Theory, which will bring with it the energy to implement change and act on the new understanding, but if the insights from Social Exchange Theory are relevant, government must recognise that trust cannot be commanded, only slowly built up as resources, structures, skills and rewards are deployed and costs and benefits at all stages and at all levels are acknowledged.

Co-operation Theory

Robert Axelrod, a political scientist, published his book *The Evolution of Co-operation* in 1984. Believing that only co-operation would ensure the survival of the species, he sought the conditions which made co-operation possible between self-interested egoists in a complex world. Axelrod made a specific use of Games Theory, that is, a mathematical theory setting out the optimum choice of strategy in conflicts of interest. Axelrod promoted a computer tournament around a game he called 'The Prisoner's Dilemma', which was a means of examining the various strategies which could be employed by people with inadequate information and different objectives when they were required to come to a decision which would bring most benefit and least harm to all the parties. Two prisoners, charged with the same crime and unable to communicate, are each separately faced with the gaoler's proposal. The gaoler suggests that if one prisoner confesses, he will go free and his confederate will be imprisoned; if *both* he and his partner confess, the sentence for both will be reduced; if *neither* confesses, the evidence will only be sufficient for a short sentence. The last option is the optimal individual strategy, but runs the risk of one confessing, leaving the other to be imprisoned. So the most co-operative strategy is for both to confess and to have a reduced sentence.

Hundreds of computer games were played and scored. Axelrod, studying the results, arrived at a strategy he called 'Tit for Tat'. This elicited behaviour which allowed both players to do better by co-operating than either did by working alone. The strategy was based on the certainty of reciprocity 'enlarging the shadow of the future'. If defection from agreement to co-operate brings retaliation, then making sure that participants recognise each other and know that they will meet again leads them to conclude that unless there is co-operative behaviour by both parties, there will not only be loss to the overall enterprise, but also to each party.

As well as reciprocity and durability of relationships, a third condition is *provocability*, that is the ability to make a quick response to uncalled-for defections. This depends on each participant having enough power in the situation to make the other realise defection, or non-co-operation, is more costly than co-operation, and that defection will be followed by the certainty, or strong probability, of punishment from the outside world.

Ideas which appear in Co-operation Theory are echoed in experience of interprofessional collaboration. Empirical research into collaboration between district nurses, general practitioners and health visitors (Bond *et al.* 1985) attempted to set out a *taxonomy of collaboration*, ranging from isolation, in which professionals never meet or communicate, to collaboration throughout an organisation in which the work of all members is fully integrated. The study rated the extent of collaboration, and found it was highest where professionals got to know a few others well and worked under such conditions that there was a strong likelihood of frequent contact. It was lowest where professionals either never met at all, or met so casually that they did not get to know each other. This finding echoes Axelrod's condition of durability, and trust contingent on evidence and history.

If the parties to co-operative enterprises do not have sufficiently equal power to reciprocate if one defects, then co-operation can degenerate into coercion.

The danger of exploitation and collusion in interprofessional collaboration where a weaker party enters the territory of a stronger without acquiring an adequate power base and not only undermines its own work but also fails adequately to represent an alternative view of society and health is discussed by Paul Bywaters (1986) in writing about medical social work in hospitals. This argues the need for *both* parties to be able to reciprocate and to be seen to be provocable, and that co-operation must not be offered unconditionally.

Co-operation Theory assumes that the parties will co-operate for their own benefit, which becomes a mutual overall gain. What if co-operation is required for the benefit of a third party, that is the client or patient? The implications of this theory are that the client should be an active not passive participant, able to assess the need for co-operation for his/her well-being, and able to reciprocate, or punish, if co-operation is not forthcoming. The delivery of health and welfare care at a very general level of control is determined through the agency of government interpreting what society considers desirable and hence, as in the policy of community care, government not individuals can be the third or proxy party requiring interprofessional collaboration. At an individual level the power of the client or patient to participate depends on the degree of choice available to him/her, that is the person's power to reciprocate or withdraw. In a market-place such power is exercised as a consumer. In public sector services, the pseudo-market creates purchasers who are agents for the users. Agents may be a fund-holding general practitioner, or a care manager in community care. Individual patients or clients may have the power to complain, but complaints processes are cumbersome and time-consuming, in the face of which organisations are often defensive. It would be a very well-informed and persistent user who alone would pursue a complaint about failures of collaboration. So such third party beneficiaries to collaboration are likely to accrue power either by being valued by their agent or by combining with others or by invoking the media.

In the idealistic 1970s Axelrod maintained that the social outcomes of co-operation transcended individual situations, and resulted in what he called 'evolutionary credit creation' with ultimate widespread benefits. Some economists (Hutton 1995) argue even in the harsher climate of the 1990s that the benefits of trustworthiness in business enterprises is seen to be effective in establishing relationships which reduce the risks of the heavy costs incurred by imperfect information and lack of commitment in short-term contracts. 'Trust is dependent upon parties to a deal caring about their reputation as moral beings and monitoring their own conduct with integrity... rewards for trustworthiness include love which becomes a means of entrenching committed behaviour'.

Co-operation Theory highlights for collaboration the recognition that it can be mutually beneficial if parties bring to it the willingness to trust the other but the power to reciprocate if the other defects. That power rests partly on the 'shadow of the future', the knowledge that any defector cannot just cut and run, but will continue to be involved in the relationship.

Conclusion

The concepts drawn from these three social theories about interaction which are relevant to a clearer understanding of collaboration in health and welfare by policy-makers, managers and professionals may be organised into three categories. All these categories are contained within the idea of competence and are therefore related to learning, which is intended to equip practitioners with competencies.

The first category is that of *attitude*. Into that falls the concept of commitment, not only to the perception of the need for collaboration, but also to the other participants and the build-up of trust and predictability. The recognition of the legitimacy of calculating costs and benefits, rather than resting on an appeal to a vague altruism is essential, as is the acknowledgement of power relationships and the differences of expectations and perspectives.

The second category is that of *knowledge*. An understanding of the common characteristics of social systems, such as boundaries, structures and processes and the concept of equifinality is necessary to effective collaboration. If participants do not know what they have to deal with in working together, and share their knowledge in terms they can all recognise and understand, they will be overcome by all the difficulties so frequently documented.

The third category is that of *skills*. The main skills which emerge are the ability to describe and map the essential elements of the relevant social network, and the ability to manage the processes of interaction between them. Such management will involve setting up appropriate structures and resources, and clarifying roles and responsibilities, as well as defining the task in terms to which all participants can subscribe, and to which people can be held accountable.

The requirement for organisations and professions to collaborate around the needs of other parties depends on a sufficiently shared perception of what is necessary, and what is to be gained. The gains may be individually different, and the perception of what is necessary may be a continuum on which professions overlap at some points. The crucial perception for interagency and interprofessional collaboration is the recognition of interdependence, and of long-term credit creation, which may benefit not only individual clients or patients, but also the professionals and their agencies, and the effective use of expensive resources in society.

CHAPTER THREE

The Dangers of Collaboration

While collaboration between Health and Social Services has been publicly encouraged in successive government papers, there has been little research or critical analysis to validate it. Much of the writing about collaboration has been mainly descriptive. If collaboration is to be effective, and to match the hopes of policy-makers and professionals, not only do the necessary conditions for success need to be elucidated, but also the dangers and the costs.

This chapter argues that collaborative enterprises need to be examined critically, in the light of the dangers and costs which might be present. The dangers arise around interests, accountability and effectiveness. Costs are often hidden, and need to be brought out into the open if collaboration is to be adequately funded.

Collaborative activities may be informal, relatively unstructured, responsive to a felt local need, often powered by a charismatic leader, or they may be policy-led, formally set up by local authorities and health authorities in accordance with government strategies such as Care in the Community. The benefits which collaboration is intended to produce are both economic and value-based. Public policy takes for granted that collaboration reduces wasteful duplication and makes more effective use of resources allocated to different agencies. It is assumed that interagency and interprofessional collaboration results in a more comprehensive response to the needs of individual patients or groups of clients, both at the planning stage and in service delivery.

Collaboration among different professionals and between different agencies is not a uniform activity. It can range from the face to face contact between a doctor and a health visitor conferring about a shared patient, to a network of professionals employed by different agencies to meet the needs of a particular client group. It can take place within a tight-knit multi-disciplinary team working under the same roof with the same patients or it can be among a group of planners, managers and professionals joining together around a common concern in a locality.

In considering what might be the dangers of collaboration, questions need to be asked. Whose interests are being served? To whom are the participants accountable? Is collaboration the most effective way of achieving the desired result?

Whose interests are being served?

Organisations usually work to ensure their own survival. In the same way it is possible that groups of professionals, joining together in good faith to work for the benefit of a particular client group or to tackle a particular social problem, find that over time they evolve a group culture, style of interaction and relationships which are so satisfying for the members who remain with the group that the group becomes an end in itself. The group which originally came together because the members were different falls into the trap of colluding to avoid the hard issues of collaboration such as differential power and status, and conflicting problem definition and incompatible priorities so that life together can be comfortable. They are satisfied that collaboration is taking place because they get on well and create a myth of togetherness. The dangers in this are of a disproportionate value being set on personal relationships, and of assuming that successful collaboration necessarily and largely depends on congenial personalities.

This emphasis on personal relationships rather than on the need for structures, for explicit skills and for the purposeful sharing of knowledge, may lead to an informal blurring of roles such that nobody is sure who is doing what and why or who should be held accountable. This confusion causes anxiety to the patient or client and hidden coercion among the members of the group in that the least powerful may give in to the prescriptive authority of the more powerful because conflict and questioning disturb the comfortable relationships.

In the attempt to make collaboration workable and satisfying, agencies and professionals can easily fail openly to acknowledge the real, legitimate differences and expectations between the participants. They may so blur roles, skills, modes of treatment and knowledge that their activity develops into a low-level genericism in which every member does a bit of everything and none of it very well, denying to clients and patients the expert skills and knowledge which each profession can deliver. It may result in a colonising or taking over by the more powerful of the tasks of the weaker professions. The result is anxiety and uncertainty, a poor delivery of service and disenchantment with collaboration itself. The masking of difference is dangerous, for difference is legitimate and necessary to represent the wholeness of individuals in complex situations. Some conflicts may seem irreconcilable; for example, care or control, except within a highly general holistic view. Different agencies and professions stand for different priorities and values, and different concepts of health and welfare, representing the necessary diversity in dynamic advanced societies and of human personality in society, so that an emphasis on freedom may conflict with the need for community, the need for dependence with the pull to independence, the call for justice and fairness with the plea for mercy and understanding. All these values find some expression in the assumptions of different professions and all need to be recognised as essential and to be negotiated.

To whom are the participants accountable?

Interagency and interprofessional collaboration without safeguards for the client or rigorous examination by the participants leads to dangers for both, and does a disservice to individuals and to society. Clients or patients individually or in groups may receive a more integrated and comprehensive service for their needs from practitioners and managers working collaboratively. But if they are unsatisfied, if all the people with whom they deal present a unified front, how do they seek redress, or how do they challenge the system? It is the poor and disadvantaged who are most dependent on the public health and welfare services and they are often the least well-equipped to challenge managers and professionals. Mechanisms of accountability to individual clients and the local community need therefore to be built into collaborative enterprises. This presents a difficulty for collaboration between local authorities with elected councillors and the health authorities with appointed members. Informal collaboration between small groups of professionals may present even more difficulty in getting redress for dissatisfied clients, because no one person may take responsibility, or be held accountable. A false consensus prevails.

Further, collaboration may not only mask legitimate difference and conflict at a personal level, but also stand in the way of formal challenge to the *status quo* of sectional interests. Work at the margins of organisations is easily sanctioned as long as resources are plentiful, and it makes no claim for redistribution. An example of this was the expansion of mental handicap services in local authorities and the NHS up until the mid-1970s, but only when resource constraints began to bite did the acute sector in the NHS need to fight to preserve its historical pre-eminence and resource allocation. The call for collaboration in the planning and delivery of care to identified client groups, without at the same time considering the need for resource reallocation, which may require redistribution, is a failure to challenge powerful interests whether they be vested in the protection afforded by the medical model of care and the appeal to clinical judgement as the final arbiter, or in social service departments allocating most resources to high-profile child care. Policy exhortation to collaboration encourages inadequate *ad hoc* growing by addition, so avoiding the need for hard thinking about priorities, purposes, resources, analysis of the balance of costs and benefits, and evaluation and accountability.

Laying unwarranted expectations on interagency and interprofessional collaboration without this hard thinking puts the blame for failure on to agencies and professionals at the local level, when it should belong to the resource allocators at government level.

Is collaboration the most effective way of addressing the desired result?

Government policies for health and welfare services have laid great emphasis on the need for collaboration to achieve comprehensive and effective meeting of need.

With the identification of care in the community as a policy, especially for elderly, mentally ill and mentally impaired people, and of social problems such as alcohol and drug abuse and Aids, there arise calls for collaboration around particular client groups and specific social issues. The danger, however, is that these new specialisms will re-enact and regroup all the factors which make collaboration difficult, not necessarily within themselves, but between themselves and the outside world. Policies which focus on a client group or a social problem, instead of on the professional and organisational delivery of skills and resources, mean only that resources are regrouped in a different way. The view is still partial and fragmented, whilst life experienced by the people served is a complex whole.

An organisational boundary around, for example, services for elderly people would serve to give identity and safety to professionals engaged within it, and to exclude those not obviously involved. On one occasion a conference on interdisciplinary work with mentally ill people attracted no health visitors, who presumably saw themselves as not relevant despite the effects of mental illness on family life. Such boundaries raise for the clients questions of entitlement and qualification. There are grey areas of gaps, into which needy clients, who don't quite fit obvious categories, fall. Boundaries may produce security and identity for the professionals, but if they become rigidly defined the service and allocation of resources fail to become responsive to the changing pattern of needs. Strategic funding such as that for community care governs the setting up of new specialist groups of agencies and professionals, but in being so specifically allocated may distort local response to local need, prevent extensions of concern into associated areas, or confine requests for resourcing to that particular budget. The knowledge base of the collaborative work may be shared within the familiar boundary but at the cost of being considered peculiar to the client group and not transferable, so that for example the professionals working together with mentally impaired people may not see that it is possible to extrapolate collaborative skills and conditions for work with other groups of clients.

Collaboration as a response to social problems, or to client groups seen as social problems, becomes part of a narrow diagnosis of cause and effect in which the prescription, that is interagency or interprofessional collaboration, springs from the perception of the main problem as being a failure to mobilise and use resources. Collaboration therefore becomes a panacea, not, as it should be, one possible response to a full analysis of needs. It becomes an easy prescription and when it is found to be difficult, because too much is expected of it and because the conditions for it are not sufficiently thought out, then yet another way of regrouping the response to problems is suggested and the process is repeated. Newer specialisms or organisations are created, and are still not the answer to the question of meeting needs. The question each time needs to be asked. Is interprofessional or interagency collaboration the most effective way of achieving the desired goal?

A study of *Young People and Heroin* (Pearson, Gilman and McIvor 1985) pointed to the 'variations in the responses and understandings of different public (and voluntary) agencies... and effort, which continue to expand in some localities without any clear sense of direction'. Informal, unstructured collaborative activities might well divert attention as well as resources from the need to make a comprehensive assessment of needs and resources within local authorities and health authorities, and thus lead to the very duplication of services and lack of rational planning which collaboration itself is intended to overcome. Such activities become sticking plaster for social wounds, and cover the need to ask questions about whether the most efficient use is being made of resources.

The danger of informal, unstructured collaborative activities is that costs are masked, costs both of time and goods such as accommodation, and that energies and enthusiasms are diverted from other objects. Even formal collaboration between statutory organisations is open to the same criticism. The report of the Audit Commission (1986) criticised the health and local authorities for preferring 'horse-trading' to joint planning and sharing resources. The costs of collaboration itself do not appear to be acknowledged formally. That there are costs is quite clear to those on whom they fall. But even the resource costs are not quantified. A District General Manager wrote: 'Experience to date has suggested that joint planning, involving as it does senior officers, is an extremely slow and time-consuming exercise and is likely to absorb a large proportion of officer time' [personal communication]. The implication is that either more staff are needed, or other responsibilities will go unmet, and there is no hint of an appreciation that joint planning could bring benefits. The disincentives to collaboration are strong.

The costs of collaborative service delivery, unless it is a recognised, resourced and formal activity, are likely to be masked within the participants' mainstream activities and therefore to be marginal and often not fully legitimised or accountable. The costs to informal carers who are an essential element in collaborative community care are, except in attendance allowances, totally unacknowledged. There is no cross-accounting for the calls on other health services which the carers, predominantly family women, make when they are under great physical or mental pressure.

As well as financial costs, there are intangible costs in collaboration. There are the opportunity costs of other work not done, but there are also the costs to organisations and professions of giving up autonomy over a defined area of concern and expertise. This leads to some experimentation and innovation, but also to mutual suspicion and mistrust, shown especially in the difficulties of joint funding, and the fear that it was a Trojan Horse infiltrating local authority programmes with central government's shifting of service patterns and provision. Collaboration also requires managers, policy-makers and professionals to adopt a system-wide thinking, a perspective very difficult for those educated to have tunnel vision, causing anxiety and a fear of being overwhelmed by the sheer weight of social need, unprotected by boundaries and categories. Collaboration seems like a very expensive giving up, an investment without direct reward. For members of collaborative enterprises to appreciate intangible benefits such as direct access to other people's managers, and gaining information from informal contacts and relationships outside the normal hierarchies at a time of acute resource constraint, means that they must be able to take a very long view of their responsibilities.

Conclusion

Raising questions about interests, accountability and costs is not to imply that experimental, pioneering or informal collaborative enterprises should not take place: only that questions of benefit, accountability and fitness for purpose should form part of continual evaluation.

Health and welfare agencies and professionals who see the need for collaboration in the delivery of health and social care and programmes for prevention should be critical of the idea of collaboration as a self-evident and desirable goal, or as a panacea, and should enter into collaboration only when it can be demonstrated to be purposeful and accountable, task-related and cost effective.

CHAPTER FOUR

Divisions and Differences within Health and Social Care

The difficulties in interprofessional and interagency collaboration have been well documented. This chapter examines some of the reasons for the differences between professions and agencies in health and social care and suggests three elements to examine, that is power, culture and structure through which the differences and divisions might be better understood by those attempting to work together. It argues that for collaboration to be firmly and realistically based it is necessary to recognise the reasons for the development of differences and the factors which reinforce them. Four responses to the differences are considered: the development of organisations, the growth of interprofessional education, teamwork, and the search for theory.

Difficulties in collaboration

Earlier writings on collaboration tended to focus on the difficulties, and the reasons behind them. A haphazard early list of the difficulties in collaboration and their causes include: 'lack of skills in communication; confusion over leadership and authority; suspicion over confidentiality; blurring of roles; lack of knowledge of other's contributions; unreal expectations; conflicting time scales; unbalanced access to resources; variable accountability; differences of class and status; opposing types of organisational structure'(Loxley 1980).

Ten years later Pietroni (1991) suggested conflicts in values and procedures; resource and agency control problems; social defences; fears of loss of control; unresolved leadership issues; differences between professions mirroring conflicts.

In the literature these difficulties continue to be recognised. Policy-makers, educationalists and trainers, special interest groups and academics have proposed various ways of addressing them, including organisational change and resource allocation, joint commissioning and management, teamworking, shared education and training and working together. Some successes are recorded, many failures. Meantime professionals can feel defensive or guilty, and agencies are criticised for being inadequate or wasteful in the face of unmet need. That collaboration can be a demanding and difficult task is not doubted. That there are differences between agencies and professions which contribute to the difficulties is obvious. If collaboration is to be a reality and not a myth, these differences need to be identified and acknowledged at all levels, so that they may be honestly faced and taken into account in assessing whether collaboration is feasible, and/or the most effective or efficient response.

Why there is division

People living in society have a range of physical, psychological, economic and social needs which they hope to meet within a web of individual and community responses. The responses are either formally or informally organised. The organisation of the responses to be effective needs to be manageable in terms of the resources available, including the human as well as the economic resources. The attempt to manage formal public responses to individual and social needs is made through social policies by governments working with established institutions, affected by particular political ideologies, and concerned with the raising and allocation of limited resources. A historical division of labour between and within health and welfare has grown up as a response to the complexity of needs, demands and resources. The divisions apparent now in health and welfare are defined in terms of the classification of client or patient, for example child care or geriatrics; methods of intervention, for example surgery or counselling; knowledge bases, for example the natural or behavioural and social services; skills, for example medical diagnosis or social care planning; organisation of service delivery, for example general practice or family centre. The range and variety of these divisions are devices for the management of complexity across the whole experience of people living in society. Because these divisions are only devices, conveniences at particular times, and because there is a tension between separation and integration, between fragmentation and wholeness in the assessment of needs and in the mobilisation of the response, the divisions are not fixed, and are always subject to change and instability.

Divisions are not static, but develop into specialisms and expertise in particular and specific knowledge and skills. The danger comes when each division ceases to recognise itself as contingent, an enabling device, but begins to consider, protect and promote its own perception, its own priorities, its own prescriptions as the whole story and to claim power and resources on that basis. The division of labour becomes dysfunctional in the meeting of health and welfare needs when the divisions, instead of being merely devices for management, become differences which lead to separation, fragmentation, isolation and a reductionist view. These consequences are then defended against question and challenge because of the power and meanings invested in them, which reflect class, status and gender divisions in society at large (Stacey 1988).

There is, therefore, a paradox to be recognised and addressed: division and boundaries are devices to make meeting need manageable in the face of complexity, but unless professions and agencies create further devices to manage the divisions and boundaries, total need will not be met. Both divisions and boundaries make sense only in terms of wholes and relationships, but they come to have implications and meanings which spread well beyond their direct utilitarian value, and reflect and have impact on the society within which they are set. Division therefore develops into difference and difference into differentials, that is relative difference, which require to be defended and perpetuated and justified because they are construed as representing values and power relationships within a society.

Collaboration is work across the boundaries, is work with difference. It challenges the safe reductionist view, the adequacy of the tunnel vision, the security of the territorial fences, the hard-won power and influence, the taken-for-granted nature of the perception. Collaboration requires communication across open boundaries, the willingness to take risks, the reciprocity of costs and gains. What works against it is the differentials within the division of labour.

Differentials in a complex society acquire a lot of the dimensions common to that society. In a primitive society differential might be measured in terms of the numbers of beads on a necklace, with people of high power and status showing it by the greatest number of beads. In a developed society the dimensions through which occupational power is demonstrated are associated with autonomy and control, dominant values and cultures, structures and organisation. These elements interact in the relationships between the people involved, but in trying to examine the differentials within the division of labour in health and welfare, to use the elements separately makes it possible to identify some of those differences which must be acknowledged and addressed if collaboration is to be effective. The differences and the associated difficulties which are illuminated by examining them in terms of power, culture and values, and structure and organisation are those which emerge from the interactions within the division of labour in health and welfare, which place the divisions in relationship to each other. The social interactions reflect the context in which collaboration has to take place. An examination of this context in terms of interrelationships and of meanings for the participant professions and agencies will lead to an understanding of the complexity of the conditions which have to be satisfied for effective collaboration.

Power as a tool for examining difference

For this purpose, power is understood in terms of sanction, control, authority and influence. Power can be recognised by asking whose will prevails, who defines the problem, whose terms are used, who controls the domain or territory, who decides upon what resources are needed and how they are allocated, who holds whom accountable, who prescribes the activity of others, and who can influence policy-makers.

The role of professionalism in the pursuit of power

One way a division or specialism may achieve power in developed societies is to attain the status of a profession. A key factor in developing the power of a profession is to establish autonomy and control over its own work (Friedson 1970). The maintenance of autonomy requires social and political influence to have a say on the state's policy and choice of issues; therefore the more issues in society can be defined in terms of the expertise of the profession, the more control the profession can exercise. A profession pursues its bid for pre-eminence by arguing that its practitioners can be trusted to put the interests of clients or patients before their own, and that their expertise enables and entitles them to know what is for the best. Professions claim to work on the basis of such a 'chivalric code' (Saks 1995) and contrast it with a business ethic of pursuing competition, profit and self-interest. Myths are created, sincerely held myths: 'A Health Service is not primarily an administrative machine, but rather a great number of personal acts of care for the sick by professionals who do not wait first to find how they will be paid' (Godber 1975).

Devices for the maintenance of autonomy are used, such as the appeal to statutory authority, or confidentiality, or specialist knowledge; 'the health and service care professions stand accused of an unjustifiable mystification and monopolisation of knowledge' (Carrier and Kendall 1995). Another weapon is the concept of 'clinical freedom', which primarily refers to individual patients or clients, but which is used more widely to support the medical profession's claim to control. In the competition in the NHS between clinicians and managers, a study of market and professional frameworks found: 'Underneath the market language remains a commitment to providing health care to the individual patient and (therefore) reliance on the authority of clinicians' (Cohen 1995).

At the same time as seeking to influence the policy of the state, a profession which has attained a large measure of autonomy seeks to defend it against the state; 'The setting of professional standards is very much a matter for the professional bodies. The main responsibility of Government is for the standards of service delivery' (Green Paper, DHSS 1986d). The difficulty of disentangling professional standards from service delivery is not identified, it is sufficient to make the ritual claim. What it actually means is: 'Give us the money without telling us how to spend it'.

The domains the professions seek to establish are subject to constant competition and challenge. The claim for territory can rest on the definition of social issues as being within the scope of the profession: for example Friedson (1970) pointed out that the control of deviant behaviour had steadily moved from the domain of the law or the church to that of medicine as such behaviour became defined as 'sick' and so requiring treatment, rather than 'bad' and requiring punishment or conversion. Sometimes the shift from one domain to another may give the new professions dubious benefits. Concern for child care has extended to the requirement for social work to control child abuse. Social work has acquired territory in which it has prime responsibility, but not the statutory power to enforce the necessary co-operation. What is then perceived as inadequate by the public, far from adding to the profession's esteem, brings it opprobrium.

Professions may therefore be in competition with each other for territory, but emphasis is growing on the right of the user to exercise influence, and if necessary, challenge. The colonisation may not be from another occupation, but from the public. In 1986 a doctor, Wendy Savage, asked: who controls childbirth? She pointed to the increasing medicalisation of birth and the rising rates of intervention, and argued for the involvement of the woman in decisions about her care, 'the role of the doctor... is that of a counsellor rather than that of an authoritarian trained professional, and this is very hard for some doctors to accept, especially the majority of male obstetricians'(Savage 1986). This example graphically illustrates the way in which the structures of professions reflect and augment the differences in status and power and gender within society.

Professional power can be augmented by using prescriptive power over other occupations, which means being powerful enough to prescribe and define what others should do, and to hold them accountable for it. The challenge to prescriptive power is reflected in familiar arguments about who should be the leader in teamwork in health care, defended by arguments resting on the very common assumption that it must be the general practitioner, on account of the legal responsibility she/he takes for the patient.

The competition for professional domain may be temporarily resolved by the establishment of yet another subdivision and specialty, for example, psycho-geriatrician, standing between psychiatry and geriatrics, or by finding a new area for the challenger. The attempt to do this can create a dilemma for professions, for as Friedson (1970) points out, 'To escape subordination to medical authority [nursing] must find some area of work over which it can claim and maintain a monopoly, but it must do so in a setting in which the central task *is* healing and controlled by medicine. That is the problem of all paraprofessions in the medical division of labour'. In the move towards higher education for qualifications in nursing and in the physical therapies there is the possibility that these professions are equipping themselves more efficiently to compete with doctors and managers, at least for some control over their own destinies. Arguments over who can prescribe are another manifestation of competition for power.

Social work, traditionally within health care facing the same dilemma of trying to establish its own domain, had to fight battles in its development, first of being considered only as administration, and then of being a profession ancillary to medicine. These challenges were fought off by anchoring social work in health care firmly in the social work profession and education, but in organisational terms it has suffered by being seen by social work management not as part of the mainstream domain, that is child and family work. It is much more secure to establish your own domain than to enter into and challenge the domain of others. The claim of social work in health care to bring exclusively a social orientation into assessment and treatment is under threat from nurses, whose new education and training calls on a greater emphasis on health, and the social factors which affect it. Such shifts and challenges may give rise to competition, or to alliances, but always to uncertainty. Nursing and social work both struggle with integration and specialisation within themselves; neither has yet established full professional status and is defensive about it; both agonise over roles and responsibilities within bureaucratic organisations. These questions of similarities and differences between two professions highlight the swaying struggle for power.

The role of the state

The state is not a disinterested, impartial player in this struggle for power, for what it does and how it does it is influenced by others, and influences them. The state intervenes in health and welfare provision for a variety of reasons, including the defence of weaker members of society, the fear of disorder, the establishment of standards and the control of cost. Different political ideologies perceive the role of the state in different ways, particularly in distinguishing between the state as a provider of services, a purchaser, or merely as a neutral arbiter. But the entry of the state automatically brings health and social care into the realm of politics because it involves the raising, the allocation and the control of funds. The need to regulate and account for costs involves a challenge to professional autonomy. The dependence of technological medicine on complex institutions, and the demographic pressures on demand, have given rise to escalating costs in health and social care throughout the developed world, and consequent calls for accountability mechanisms as part of the pursuit of cost containment. In the NHS these are being carried out through an emphasis on corporate rational planning, a greater emphasis on managerialism and the introduction of competition and market forces. New occupations and professions enter the arena and compete for influence and control, as a direct result of the state's involvement. 'The fundamental question is whether managers possess special knowledge which both they and clinicians feel to be valid and worthy of [the same] respect as medical knowledge' (Cohen 1995). That is a fundamental question only because specialist knowledge is seen as a route to establishing power, because if it is specialist it is exclusive. It is powerful, however, only if it can influence the agenda and be seen to be relevant.

The state also pays professionals in the public sector, and the different ways of remunerating different professions create obstacles to understanding and working together. The system whereby general practitioners augment their income around payments for items of service and complex allowances results in professional income made up of a multitude of small financial calculations and incentives. This can create an entrepreneurial attitude, and consequent suspicion between the so-called independently contracted practitioner and other salaried professionals such as nurses, paramedicals and social workers who work within a system which frees them from immediate financial considerations, either of cost or reward, but generally pays them less.

The notion of the client or patient as 'customer' or 'consumer' pervades much of the new managerialism and the emphasis on market mechanisms, but generally the power of the citizen as patient or client in relation to health care tends to be exercised through proxy professionals, or is subordinate to the power of the professionals, partly because most people move in and out of the health care system infrequently, while for the professionals it is their occupational domain. The idea of customer, even consumer, is far too simplistic. Health is not a product to be bought or not as the customer chooses. The managerialist market view of the patient or client is a misconception derived from an economic model and the consumer movement where choice rests on comprehensive information. Health is an experience and a characteristic of each individual, not the independent product of a professional's activity, to be priced and marketed as a consumer durable. Nevertheless, while most professional and lay contacts in health and social services in this country take place in a corporate publicly funded context accountable to the state, clients or patients in their role as citizens corporately do need to be satisfied. Power as a concept for examining the differences between the divisions of labour in the delivery of health and social care therefore illuminates the ever-changing, shifting pattern of dominance, alliances and conflict as élites struggle to establish and maintain their autonomy and control, and new groupings arise to challenge them. Attempts at collaboration, if they are to succeed, must be viewed in the light of this fluid scene; nothing is given or permanent. But the acknowledgement and recognition of the part power plays in establishing autonomy, in the allocation of resources, the marking out of domains, the claims to authority and expertise, and in its reflection of power in society is crucial to an understanding of the necessary conditions for collaborative endeavours.

'Culture' as a tool for examining difference

One way in which professional groups seek to sustain their power is by developing and sustaining an occupational culture which influences and identifies its members as distinct from those of other groups. An occupational culture is that collection of shared assumptions, custom and practice, models of reality which mark out the boundaries between those who belong inside and those others who are outside. The members share a set of priorities and values, which probably include the stereotyping of others outside, especially others who are in competition for domain, power and resources. Part of such a culture is a system of values which the group espouses, and on which it rests its claim to validity and authority. Culture and values are therefore further concepts interwoven with the concept of power in understanding how divisions of labour in health and welfare care have established and reinforced difference, and marked out differentials between the divisions.

The building of an occupational culture

The culture of a professional group is closely bound up with its identity as seen through the eyes of its adherents or its critics or society at large. When the group identity can draw into itself attributes such as trustworthiness, expertise, wisdom, then it will acquire esteem and enhance the self-esteem of its members. If a group is felt to have negative attributes and the members themselves accept these, then that group's public and self-esteem will be low and it will be judged to be weak. A professional group's identity and esteem will interact with the individual identities and self-esteem of its members so that in certain aspects of their lives the social and the individual identities merge and new members will join the group because they perceive in it an identity to which they aspire.

The professional group's identity will be reinforced during the course of training by the socialisation that takes place from the interaction of peers and the examples of seniors, and will be maintained in the course of a professional career by various social mechanisms. Among these mechanisms are the establishment of norms for the group, the use of myths which tell the story of the group, the frames of reference through which its members perceive the world and according to which they agree priorities and courses of action, and the defences which enable the group and its members to cope in the face of challenge and threat. All these mechanisms interact to reinforce each other, and so maintain a corporate ethos. The establishment of professional identity is necessary for confidence and clarity in role, and as the basis for interaction with others. Without it there is blurring and confusion.

The norms of a group determine what is taken-for-granted, expected, acceptable behaviour, language, presentation, styles of management and decision-making. These norms are rarely exposed to criticism from people outside. Shared assumptions build up into myths about the professional group, which serve to reinforce the mutuality of the members and the control of internal conflict. Such myths in different groups which may be required to work together with another can cause mutual incomprehension. Doctors tend to emphasise medical autonomy and self-reliance, while social workers value mutual support and acknowledge the influence of group dynamics. The myths affect the perceptions of the group members of their own way of behaving, which is judged to be desirable, and that of others, especially others who may be suspected of challenging or competing for power, which is judged to be irrelevant, incompetent, or even hostile.

The perceptions used by a professional group are drawn from the professional frames of reference which rest on beliefs about the way things work, about people and their relationships. They inform questions and decisions about what is relevant information and which are the priorities, tasks and methods seen as appropriate for members of the group. A group's frame of reference may be used to evaluate that of other groups and often places the role of members of another group in a very different position in relation to a situation than the position in which those people would place themselves; this will reflect the probably unacknowledged competition between the groups. One study of social workers and general practitioners (Bell 1986) found that the social workers generally felt that the general practitioners made too many 'practical' that is, low-grade demands, and one doctor complained that 'the attached social workers see themselves doing case work and psychotherapy only. Some GPs prefer to do this kind of work themselves, or refer patients to highly trained and experienced colleagues'. The fact that increasing numbers of general practices use attached counsellors, either directly or from a voluntary agency, suggests that such staff are not seen as an occupational or professional threat but as part of the general practice's range of resources and under its control. Difficulty arises when the value placed on others is seen solely in terms of the professional group's own frame of reference; as, for example, a consultant psychiatrist at an appointments panel for a hospital manager asked well-qualified applicants, 'Are you going to get us more money?'(personal communication). Such clashes, if their sources are not recognised, will give rise to mutual incomprehension and often hostility. More seriously, if the frames of reference are too exclusive much ill-health goes untreated because it does not present in an orthodox way and many social needs may be passed over or perceived as trivia by doctors untrained to respond or to refer. Similarly, an emphasis on social circumstances which does not recognise the impact of ill-health will also do the client a disservice and fail to draw in relevant skills.

Defences

In the same way in which individuals can be described as defending their self-esteem and equilibrium against anxiety, which might otherwise be overwhelming, so too can the behaviour of members of professional groups be explained. People working in health and social care from whatever profession are frequently required to cope in situations of extreme distress and suffering: professional ethos and training are intended to equip practitioners to respond without being overwhelmed.

Psychological defences against anxiety which enable professionals to cope can be positive but defences may be maladaptive if they prevent other needs being recognised or other resources being recruited. Defences function to make the response to anxiety manageable, and within a professional frame of reference situations which can be reframed or understood in recognisable terms become manageable within the armoury of the profession. But some social situations are experienced as so overwhelming that they can only be responded to by projecting the impotence outside, either on to the patient or client or on to particular personalities or another associated professional group or another agency. Suspicion, avoidance, scapegoating, stereotyping, denial, blaming, self-idealisation are all common defence mechanisms in the interchange between professions involved in individual or social distress. They are adaptive in the sense that each profession is thereby enabled either to make some response or excuse its own helplessness but they are maladaptive in that they often prevent appropriate referral or appropriate recruitment of resources. In terms of individual and group identity, defence mechanisms can be seen as having a purpose, but if they become destructive myths, they need to be challenged and replaced in the interests of a total response to need. The Tavistock Institute of Human Relations (Obholzer and Roberts 1994) works with small groups of people from organisations to help them see for themselves how personal, interpersonal and organisational systems interact and how irrationality in one sphere can trigger it in another. It is argued that by bringing such influences to light anxieties can be creatively and not destructively contained and effectiveness fostered.

Values

The values of professional groups develop from their history and their shared assumptions. Different professional groups identify themselves with different values and different priorities, each group tempted to take them for granted and claim that theirs is the only valid world view. To recognise that different value systems are interwoven and each is only partial is to acknowledge uncertainty. Such acknowledgement requires flexibility and responsiveness, rather than resting unquestioningly in certainties which may be limited, although they serve to reinforce self-esteem.

Values in different professional and agencies may be assumed to be in opposition but in reality they are aspects of wholes, and need to be in dialogue. They are not simple dualities. The emphasis on the needs of the individual is as essential to the well-being of society as is the emphasis on the needs of the group; the recognition of collegiality as an organising principle is no less valuable than the adherence to hierarchy; the judgement of the individual practitioner as the basis for the allocation of resources is not paramount over the accountability to society for the use of social resources; the responsibility taken by a professional is not more important than the procedures decided upon within a bureaucracy. All these values, current within the debates in the health and welfare system, are contestable; each must be argued for afresh and continually challenged if powerful groups are not to assert one set of values as always dominant, whatever the material or psycho-social cost. The appeal to 'clinical judgement' can be used to colonise social needs; ideological righteousness can be blind; managerial efficiency can be heartless.

The role of the state is not valueless, and will serve to reinforce or ignore values espoused by groups within the health and social care system, or by subgroups within the professions. The emphasis on welfarism or on market forces will make it more or less difficult for particular groups to argue their case: for example, social work with its history of work with the poor and deprived will find it harder to justify its claims for resources when a government emphasises non-intervention than when it upholds corporate responsibility, and when recipients are stigmatised as undeserving their lack of esteem reflects on those who work with them.

The dangers of professional cultures

Professional groups develop and maintain an identity for themselves which rests on a culture composed of values, attitudes, myths, norms, defences and frames of reference. The danger is that these professional identities, being associated with the maintenance of power by those who benefit from it, are therefore essentially conservative in the sense that they are resistant to any change which may threaten the balance of power. Weaker groups will try to pursue change which strengthens them but when they have attained it are likely to become equally subject to the forces of inertia and protectionism, for the sake, for example, of investment in current career patterns. Such conservatism may in fact become exploitative of the rest of society and when that exploitation becomes exposed so it gives rise to a countervailing force. For example, when the uncosted use of resources by the medical profession became exposed as concerns about costs in the NHS grew, so a countervailing force was brought into play to control it. The development of managerialism and market mechanisms in the NHS are examples of attempts to bring about necessary change which a powerful profession had been unable to do or indeed to acknowledge.

These battles are played out in the structures of the health and welfare system. Struggle to bring about change which is more than peripheral or additional and which therefore cannot be incorporated within the existing culture or frames of reference without challenging them is experienced as threatening. It requires an arduous reframing of so many of the elements which make up the professional group's world view and a destabilising of the myths and values on which security and esteem have rested. This is especially true when such change is imposed from outside, either from the managerialism required by the government within the NHS, or from the pressure of public concern as for example in relation to child abuse and the consequences for the priorities of the social services. Professional culture, values, identity and frames of reference are always subject to negotiation within and without as the professional group is judged to be serving not only its own interests but those of society, according to how those interests are construed by policy-makers and resource allocators. Professions are foolish to assume that they are above challenge, and would be wise to anticipate change before it is forced upon them. If the medical profession, especially in hospitals, had in the 1970s and 1980s taken seriously and acted upon the need for widespread medical audit and accountability, instead of shroud-waving, it might have been better equipped to counter the rise of managerialism and the market doctrines of the Radical Right (Timmins 1995). The difficulty is of course that large professions are not homogenous groups, but a collection of rivalries and alliances like the world outside.

Structure and organisation as tools for examining difference

Professions are not monolithic organisations with all members equal in status or influence. They have within them subgroups of higher or lower status. This status reflects and interacts with relative status in society, shown in factors such as income, length of training and specialist qualifications. In a dominant occupational culture some subgroups are seen as less influential so that, for example, community physicians, unable to prescribe or appeal to 'clinical judgement', and general practitioners sharing disputed territory with community nurses and social workers, have lower status than do hospital consultants, and within the hospital sector the service givers such as pathologists and anaesthetists have a lower status than do physicians or surgeons.

Nursing, traditionally organised in a rigid hierarchy, allocates status according to the position in the hierarchy, but also to the length of training, level of qualification, and to the status of the associated medical speciality, for example intensive care or geriatrics. Health visitors with their separate origins and degree of autonomy in their work have maintained a higher status and midwives see themselves as even more separate and self-governing, seeking to defend these precious identities against educational changes in nursing at large.

Social work, historically developed at different times as separate groups organised around client populations and specialist training, integrated into one profession in 1970 with the establishment of a professional body, the British Association of Social Work, the setting up of the large social service departments, and generic training in higher education. Despite the ideal of generic work on which this integration was based and the emphasis on generic training, specialisms have re-emerged over the years since 1970. Statutory obligations and pressure for child care have made work with children and families the dominant concern, so down-grading, or rather never up-grading, work with elderly people or mentally impaired people. Under the stress of increasing demand and public awareness of child abuse and of constrained local government finance, resources are pulled into this dominant area even from previously high-status professional subgroups, the medical and psychiatric social workers. These subgroups were weakened by being marginalised in the formal structures of the National Health Service reorganisation in 1974 when their position as employees of the NHS was lost, and they became employed by the social service departments. The base within the local authority strengthened their social work professional identity, but within the culture of social service departments medical and psychiatric social workers suffer the disadvantages of being associated with an alien organisation; they are often stereotyped as being subject to the domination of a medical model of care, if not actually to the authority of a more powerful profession. These two subgroups were therefore perceived as personifying a threat to the autonomy which a developing profession seeks, and at the same time were resented because of the reflection from the higher social status of the medical profession. The emphasis on assessment for care plans for community care on discharge from hospital has strengthened medical social work in one aspect of its role but at the expense of its contribution to treatment and rehabilitation.

Real resource ambiguities are also present in funding a social work service to teaching or specialist hospitals whose patients may be drawn from all over the country, while the allocation of social work service funding is the responsibility of the often hard-pressed local authority in whose boundaries the hospitals are set, and whose own social service department serves only its own local population. Thus it may be seen that differences within professions may be exacerbated by the formal structures.

A local authority is a multi-issue organisation including a great range of professional groups, and a health authority or a trust hospital or a general practitioner practice are basically mono-issue organisations with a limited variety of professions, one of them dominant. This difference affects the way in which people working within the organisations behave and the different tensions they work under. All organisations are coalitions of occupational groups gathered together to perform a range of tasks. There may be as much competition between professions working within the same organisation as between those in different agencies. Each group seeks to use the organisation to protect its own interests. The differences between professional groups and agencies are played out within the structures, and mutual incomprehension and suspicion continue to manifest themselves alongside real efforts to work together.

The new management ethos in the NHS, with its expectation of the rational allocation of resources and cost-effectiveness, and decision-making set according to a particular place in a management structure, sits uncomfortably and often uncomprehendingly with expectations of collegiate relationships, professional autonomy, discretion and values. This tension is experienced by hospital doctors expected to account for their use of resources within an allocated annual cash-limited budget or budget-holding general practitioners making decisions on the basis of funds available and exercising purchasing power. Social workers within beleaguered local authorities afraid of public opprobrium find themselves increasingly subject to directives and formal procedures.

General practitioners, despite their relatively low status within the medical profession because of the location of their work and its generalist, gatekeeping nature, continue to enjoy for the time being the freedom of a fragmented structure with an independent contractor remuneration. The distinction within general practice between budget holders and non-budget holders following the 1990 NHS and Community Care Act created a difference of power and influence within the specialism, a difference whose implications have yet to be worked through.

The professions jockey for position in the new forms of service delivery. Primary health care is as yet an aspiration, perhaps an ideology, rather than an organisation, but lines are drawn up between general practitioners and community nurses to claim it as their domain although the concept of teamwork is used to avoid the necessary conflict. Community care is supported by statute but so far it has failed to deliver the desired quality of care at a lower cost except by transferring costs to the informal sector. Individual needs-based programmes are still constrained by resources and by limitations placed on public sector provision in favour of the private sector.

The picture therefore is confused; the professions all share a social context and experience the common pressures within it, despite their different organisations. The agencies within which the professions work are themselves complex and subject to conflicting pressures. The professions are not homogenous monoliths, and especially from inside experience themselves as unstable. The new management ethos, the emphasis on market forces, budgets and financial constraints present a common challenge to both health and welfare professionals.

What professions have in common therefore is that they all possess power to a greater or lesser degree. They all experience a professional culture which contains sets of assumptions and values, particular language and expectations, and helps to give them an identity which enables them to function in the face of the demands made upon them. Professionals all work within structures and organisations, even within agencies, experiencing constraints and opportunities. All this is held in common.

The differences are defined by the boundaries within and between professional groups, which are both symbolic in terms of culture and perceived power and real in terms of agency structures and actual power. There is, therefore, division. But to deliver an adequate, comprehensive and defensible service to people in complex situations, agencies and professions need to combine. This dilemma is exacerbated because the divisions acquire other dimensions.

Differentiation

The division of labour in health and welfare has developed historically, in pursuit of in-depth knowledge and skills at more and more specialised levels, and with the associated organisation of resources and power. At the same time there has grown the recognition that human need cannot be segmented and portions treated in isolation, but that needs interact so as to affect the way in which they are experienced. The complexity and diversity is so great that no one professional can respond completely alone. The attempt to do so results either in a very partial response, or in a vague and low-skilled generalism, which loses the benefit of specialism and its hard-won knowledge and skills. The only true generalist is the person actually in need in his or her situations in that from that perspective all the needs are experienced, even though even that person may require help to identify what the needs are and not just to accept the definition given by the first professional called upon.

The division of labour rests on difference and diversity. The difference and diversity express and reflect social public issues; they stand for choices; they identify values such as individual responsibility or group accountability, the tension between needs and rights, integration and separation. The different professions, and subdivisions within them, are perceived as taking stances to defend contestable concepts, that is, ideas and experiences all of which need to be expressed and argued so that they can be recognised and valued and remain in creative dialogue.

The division of labour because it serves a totality either of an individual, a community or a society, itself implies both independence and dependence. The more complete the division of labour, the more interdependent the parts become on each other not only to meet the needs of the whole but also to survive, because each part needs to be serviced and supported by other parts in the complex organisation of a society. Although division of labour arises because of difference and complexity, the difference and complexity do not in themselves create difficulty. It is when the divisions seek to differentiate and protect themselves by organising, seeking autonomy, power and influence, and defending their identity by establishing dominant cultures and values that conflict and competition arise. It is the differentiation, the distance between professions, not the division which makes collaboration difficult. It is because of the differentiations in society that working together becomes not a straightforward co-operation but a disappointing or fraught experience. The differentiations dominate our expectations and experience and we forget that the division of labour is a device for making complexity manageable.

Too often the enthusiasm for collaboration or requirement to collaborate ignores the differentiations which have arisen around the division of labour. The social differentiations may be modified, may change, but they are deep-rooted in society and therefore in the organisation of health and social care in society. To expect profession or agencies to collaborate as if such differentiations did not exist is naïve and self-defeating.

Response to division and difference

In parallel to developments in public policy, which were intended to bridge the divide between health and welfare organisations by exhortation, structures, funding, joint work and commending education and planning, professional bodies and their educational arms have also moved to close the gap. Some of this work has been done through coalitions of formal organisations coming together around fields of activity, such as primary health and community care, around the need for interprofessional or interagency education, or around particular client groups such as mentally impaired people. Some of this work has been done by clusters of enthusiastic individuals, possibly developing into recognised bodies. One response therefore has been the development of interprofessional organisations to promote interprofessional and interagency practice and education. Second, the growth of interprofessional education itself as a major activity intended to bridge the divide is to be considered. Third, one of the pressures toward the development of education is the emphasis on teamwork, especially in general practice, as a device for co-ordinating interprofessional work. And fourth, as education and organisation have expanded, so have the publications. It has been recognised that collaborative practice and education lack a theoretical base, but as academics and teachers have studied and written up what has happened, the search for theory has begun.

The evolution of organisations

The formal interest of professional and training bodies in co-operation and collaboration between services followed the setting up, under the Health Visitors and Social Workers Training Act 1962, of councils for education and training. (Thwaites 1993). The climate of opinion at that time was in favour of co-ordination and genericism, as seen in the Seebohm Report on the Social Services of 1968 and in 1973 the NHS Reorganisation Act to enable integration and co-ordination. Under the auspices of the Royal College of General Practitioners, the Council for the Education and Training of Health Visitors and the then Institute for Social Work Training, in 1972 a seminar was held in Windsor for recently qualified staff and an influential report was published (Bennett, Dewar and Dick 1972) in the Journal of the Royal College of General Practitioners.

In 1979 the Central Council for Education and Training in Social Work, the Council for the Education and Training of Health Visitors and the Royal College of General Practitioners, newly joined by the Panel of Assessors for District Nurse Training, organised a Symposium on Interprofessional Learning in Nottingham. This 'represented a landmark in interprofessional collabora-tion... a unique... collaborative effort between the four national bodies... and demonstrated publicly for the first time the policy of these organisations in encouraging interprofessional learning' (Flack 1980). Following the sympo-sium there were joint workshops at local and regional levels and a standing group representing the professions of social work, district nursing, general medical practice and health visiting was formed. A report on the development of interprofessional education and training for members of primary health care teams was published by this standing group in 1983. In that year the separate branches of nursing were absorbed into the United Kingdom Central Council.

One of the members of the standing group was Marian Strehlow, previously from CETHV. In 1984 she chaired a national conference organised at Middlesex Polytechnic by a general practice vocational trainer, a nurse educator and a social work lecturer, who had been running joint short courses each summer for three years for their students. The conference attracted over 60 participants and, at its end, set up a small working party to see how Marian Strehlow's exhortation 'to act together and move forward' could be obeyed (Loxley 1984). This was the origin of the Centre for the Advancement of Interprofessional

Education, now a major player in the field, and demonstrates how developments depend on what has gone before and do not spring up out of nothing.

The emphasis of the earlier work around interprofessional collaboration and education was an attempt to influence opinion primarily among educators and to encourage joint training courses, although these were largely isolated and localised. From the 1980s there was a shift of gear. The large training bodies no longer took the lead through coalitions promoting special events, but instead set up within themselves small groups with a particular remit and recruiting others representing different professions, or gave their support to organisations which sprang up as a result of this work of dedicated enthusiasts. By 1995 there were 11 United Kingdom National Co-ordinating Bodies founded between 1987 and 1995. (See Appendix B.) Their growth has been haphazard and uncoordinated, leading to overlap. But despite this these newer bodies have become more proactive than the earlier coalitions. As well as seeking to influence opinion among educationalists they proclaim their more definite purpose of developing and promoting interprofessional and interagency practice and education. At the same time in Europe in 1987 the European Network for the Development of Multi-Professional education in Health Sciences was set up, following two preparatory sessions in 1984 and 1986. Its aim is to support the implementation of multi-professional education, to spread information and encourage evaluation and the possibility of collaborative research.

The means employed among all these bodies include promoting research, developing data-banks, organising seminars, conferences, workshops, combining with others to speak to policy-makers, publishing newsletters and bulletins, recruiting members, building national and regional networks of practitioners and educators, and seeking support from influential bodies such as the professional associations, the Department of Health, the King's Fund, and influential individuals such as the Prince of Wales.

The organisational development of the Centre for Advancement in Interprofessional Education (CAIPE) demonstrates some of the key factors in survival. From a small group of individual enthusiasts to an organisation with an annual budget of £95,000 (1994–95) it has passed through various stages. At the beginning it established its key principle of being in balance interprofessionally, and not allowing itself to run the risk of being dominated by one profession. This has continued to govern its choice of locations, and search for funding. From the original small nucleus meeting in a basement at the King's Fund College, it was awarded seed funding from the King's Fund Centre, which included hospitality and support services for three years. In 1991 it then moved, having succeeded in gaining financial backing from a range of charitable sources, to what was deemed to be a professionally neutral but academically prestigious site, the London School of Economics. At this stage it was also able to employ a part-time director. The shift from being run by enthusiastic volunteers taking time from their main employment to being an employer proved a difficult transition, compounded by confusions over role and obligations with the academic host. In 1992 CAIPE gained charitable status but the need to have trustees as well as a director in addition to a council put more strain on the developing organisation. These strains were resolved in 1994 with a change of staff to a full-time salaried director and a move to a base giving more freedom from the host. A major factor in CAIPE's success has been stability among the executive members from the beginning and the commitment of a chairman, now president, Dr John Horder, who was able to give the developing organisation a great deal of his time and prestige. CAIPE is still evolving as it moves toward its second decade and only finance could put its future in doubt. Its functions are expanding and its credibility growing.

The context for the founding and development of co-ordinating organisations in primary health and community care since the mid 1980s has not been easy. The major difficulty has been precarious funding and the need to compete with each other for scarce resources. This competition not only for funds but for influence, for members, for supporters, for role and identity, has mirrored the difficulties of collaboration itself. 'The pressure of raising funds leads to the proposition that bodies [seeking] to promote collaboration would first have to apply the principle to themselves'. (Leathard 1994). The experience of competition for CAIPE, for example, has been not only with the outside world, but also between itself and its members as money-raising projects and research have been in contention. These conflicts emerge periodically, but attempts to deal with them are made by bringing them out into the open, defining and reiterating roles, and finding some regulatory means of anticipating or resolving conflict. The commitments and goodwill mean that members are prepared to work at working together, the gain of remaining being greater than the gain of seceding.

Organisations such as those listed are important not just because they undertake work, but because they provide a focus, an identity, for an important issue. Interprofessional and interagency collaboration is a frail enterprise. It is at the margins of the major professional concerns and therefore vulnerable to pressure. Unless such organisations give this cause a presence and a voice, it could easily die.

Interprofessional education and training

Education and training which includes members of two or more professions learning together has been long and widely held as an essential component of collaboration. In 1979 the Nottingham Symposium was entitled 'Education for Co-operation in Health & Social Work'. In 1988 a World Health Organisation Report *Learning to Work Together for Health* found multi-professional education already an established part of postgraduate and continuing education in Europe. In this country there have been a few consistent contributors. A paper in 1993 outlined 20 years of development at the Postgraduate Medical School at Exeter University (Pereira Gray *et al.* 1993). The Marylebone Centre Trust, established in 1988, set up its Education & Training Unit which built on previous informal experience and later developed links with Westminster University.

Such dedicated organisations apart, the development in the UK of interprofessional education, although widespread, has been varied, haphazard and localised. Two national surveys by the Centre for the Advancement of Interprofessional Education (Shakespeare *et al.* 1989; Barr and Waterton 1996) found, in 1988, 695 examples and in 1993–94, 655 run from a wide range of agencies, including schools of nursing, voluntary organisations, institutions of further and higher education and workplaces. The courses ranged widely in the number of participants and in their duration, and although many were evaluated, they were not accredited apart from those in the second survey which were part of modular programmes and some of those run by the Open University.

Professional and Training Bodies and special interest groups have also seen interprofessional education and training as part of their remit, either by supporting and encouraging short courses or by organising conferences, seminars and workshops intended to equip practitioners, educators and policy-makers with information and give them opportunities to meet around common concerns.

More recently there has been a growth in accredited Masters' Courses in institutions of higher education, other than postgraduate medical centres. A study (Storrie 1992) of 12 institutions offering such courses found that only one (Exeter) was established before 1990 and since the study there have been many more. (CAIPE Databank). These developments may indicate that this field is becoming 'an accepted and respected academic activity' (Storrie 1992).

Nevertheless, there are questions to be raised about interprofessional education. The assumptions behind it seem to be twofold. The goal may be that learning to work together will result in a more efficient and more responsive service; but one driving force seems to be well-documented difficulties of interprofessional collaboration, and it is assumed first that negative experiences may be overcome or anticipated by positive ones of interaction in an educational setting, and second that collaborative skills will come about through a sort of osmosis as professionals learn at the same time about a particular client group, or policy changes, or new organisations. A study (Loxley 1980) found that collaboration as a topic was rarely addressed in its own right and similarly 12 years later Storrie (1992) found there was little evidence in the Masters' Courses of an explicit commitment to the promotion of teamwork and co-operation, except for the courses then in the planning from South Bank University and the Marylebone Centre.

The translation into training experiences of these two assumptions – that the difficulties can be addressed through small post-qualifying learning experiences, and that collaboration will be best experienced by learning with, from and about each other around topics of common concern, link up with a further assumption that there is a common core of knowledge and a common range of skills which may be acquired during training. The search for these commonalities is formalised in National Vocational Qualifications programmes and the pursuit of occupational standards (EL(95) 84), so that a common language and common methodology may be established to link support workers and professional education and training. Unless interprofessional education can get beyond its common-sense assumption that talking together can lead to knowledge can lead to understanding can lead to respect and liking which is transferable, then it could be overtaken. 'Advocates and architects of interprofessional education will need to assert its distinctive characteristics, qualitatively and operationally as much as conceptually' (Barr 1994).

A further threat to professional control of interprofessional education courses comes from the changes in the organisation of health and welfare and the emphasis within the Department of Health on the breaking down of old demarcation lines (Rogers 1995) within the NHS Executive itself, and across old patterns of work-force planning by profession to new local consortia of the employers of health care professionals which will commission education and training direct with education providers. Education will become employment driven, 'rooted in the realities of service need', with conjoint professional qualifications based on a common language. Unless the health and welfare professions can demonstrate that interprofessional collaboration can be taught in overt ways which can be qualitatively assessed and that it can be effectively exercised for the benefit of users as perceived by their proxies, then the way will be left open to the promotion of a core worker at a common but probably low-grade level of expertise, who will be cheaper to employ, but not able to offer the benefits of mobilising a range of specialised expertise within the division of labour.

Interprofessional education and training has been an accepted way of responding to the differences and divisions within the health and welfare field; it has been the focus of a lot of activity, and taken a lot of energy. It needs however to be recognised not as an end in itself but as a necessary if insufficient condition for effective collaboration. At one level it should address current service development, emphasising current competence and efficiency, but at another be seen as an ongoing professional education aiming to promote understanding, innovation and effectiveness. The establishment of a generic therapist or core worker places integration as the main component of one occupational group; it would still not resolve the difficult question of co-ordination across the division of labour and agencies in health and welfare. Interprofessional education needs a conceptual framework against which it can assess itself, and against which it can be measured, to justify and resource it.

Teamwork

The emphasis in much of the literature on collaboration in health and welfare, and in the educational programmes intended to enhance it, is on teamwork. This is particularly so when doctors either locally or through the Royal College of General Practitioners are involved and the key concept then is the primary health care team. Co-ordination within groups of similarly qualified professionals is not new in either health or welfare, but the concern with the idea of teams including differently qualified workers began in the 1960s. It has a double genesis, in both social work and general practice.

In social work the exploration into the justification and practice of mixed teamwork began in the USA (Brieland, Briggs and Levenberger 1973), driven by the rise of new social welfare agencies responding to the civil rights and anti-poverty movements, and by mental health programmes moving into the community. There was a shortage of professionally qualified social workers to staff these agencies, and their traditional one-to-one casework was not seen as universally appropriate. Non-professionals were employed, and given on-the-job training. Questions began to be raised about levels of competence. There was a perceived threat to professional control and authority. At the same time philosophical justifications as well as pragmatic ones for the idea of teamwork were found in the growth of holistic models and their emphasis on making a comprehensive response to the patients' or clients' needs. The answer to both the threat to professional authority and to the goal of putting the client at the centre was to experiment with teamwork as a way of organising mixed staff and making best use of qualified social workers as team leaders, who would manage, supervise and co-ordinate as well as being involved with the more complex cases.

Such ideas from the USA were influential in this country and coloured the organisation of the large social services departments from 1970 onward, with the setting up of generic social work teams to serve a neighbourhood or a patch, and the later evolution of more specialised teams organised around a particular client group, and containing social work professionals at different levels of experience, other professionals such as occupational therapists, and non-professionals.

In general practice, questions of team began to be raised with the development of health centres. The idea of teamwork received an impetus with the attachment of district nurses and health visitors to individual general medical practitioners during the 1960s. The term 'primary health care team' first appeared formally in the DHSS Annual Report of 1974 but much developmental work had already gone on with the encouragement of the Royal College of General Practitioners (Horder 1994). Statutory funding for the employment of a range of staff in general practices has enabled a widespread growth of primary health care teams, further encouraged by the setting up of budget-holding general practices. Such teams would now be seen typically to include general practitioners and practice nurses, practice managers and clerks and receptionists, plus possible attachments of community nurses, very occasionally social workers, and sometimes access to dietitians and physical therapists and the occasional employment of counsellors.

The growth of teamwork in primary health care very early on gave rise to calls for training (Horder 1995) as the difficulties in co-ordination began to be recognised and addressed. Teams have been much studied and described, and definitions, typologies, taxonomies, and metaphors abound, from sport to anatomy, in attempts to understand the implications of structure and process. Co-ordinating bodies have been founded (Appendix B) to bring together not the members of individual teams but their representative occupational, professional or educational bodies to influence policy and education by acting together.

Not in social work, where there seems to be far less formal concern about teamwork, but in general practice, questions have been raised about the reality of primary health care teams. 'Teamwork', like 'co-operation' and 'collaboration', is a word in regular use in policy documents and educational promotion as a self-evidently desirable goal and method, the key to greater efficiency and more effective service. The question is asked, however: is the team a myth? (Horder 1995). Is it a cosy word which everyone can cheer and in the cheering avoid the hard questions? The appeal to 'teamwork', like the appeal to collaborate, is largely rhetorical, and it is therefore necessary to try and understand the purposes the rhetoric is serving. It creates a symbol or device which helps to make a complex and confusing task seem more manageable. Organisation Theory examines such symbols (Belman and Deal 1984), and suggests that they are created to reduce ambiguity, resolve confusion, increase predictability and provide direction, especially where goals and methods are uncertain and unclear. Devices such as the appeal to teamwork lead to a set of ideas and assumptions which stretch over boundaries between different disciplines and which different agencies, occupations and professions can shelter under. The result is to try and resolve interagency and interprofessional conflicts by fudging questions of power and competition. The appeal to teamwork, just as the appeal to collaboration, enables policy-makers to avoid the crucial issues of irreconcilable structures and limited resources by laying on practitioners the responsibility of mitigating their effects, and practitioners can accept it without fully understanding or recognising that it contains unresolved contradictions. The myth serves to disguise the reality with an appealing ideology.

The danger spreads to the idea of collaboration and to that of interprofessional education in health and welfare. Teamwork is treated as if it were synonymous with collaboration, as if it were the prime if not the only way of organising. In primary health care teams where there is agreement among the members about the importance of the total enterprise, that is medicine, and there is a clear demarcation of roles and authority based on professional status and structures, then the task is not that of collaboration but of co-ordination within a mono-issue agency. It is only when members of the team go outside and have to relate to professionals from other agencies who do not subscribe to the same priorities or assumptions that they face conflict and a lack of consensus. The independent contractor trained to exercise independent judgement and autonomy finds it difficult to share.

One area of evidence for this assessment is interprofessional education for health and welfare. Again and again the low participation rate of general practitioners in courses not based in their work or professional settings has been noted (Loxley 1980; Storrie 1992; Barr and Waterton 1996). The reasons for this lack of participation may be personal, or practical, or structural, or professional, or educational. The reverse is seen in the high level of participation of nurses in interprofessional education. What is the gain of such courses to the professional? Who pays? How much time is available? How relevant are courses to needs? None of these questions has been studied.

A meeting at the Royal College of General Practitioners, 1994, of senior doctors and policy-makers (Horder 1995) considered that continuing education including interprofessional education to be relevant and successful needed to be linked to practice or service developments. This harmonises with the ideology of adult learning which influences most attempts at interprofessional education and stresses the need for such learning to be task and problem orientated.

Nevertheless, although perceived relevance is obviously desirable, there is a danger that such programmes may become only training, very much focused on the here and now, very practical and anti-intellectual. Understanding, innovation, transferability and flexibility may not be valued, and reaching out beyond what is already known may be too frightening.

The emphasis on teamwork and on the primary health care team in particular in the literature on collaboration and on interprofessional education needs clear scrutiny. Without such scrutiny there may well continue to be two parallel tracks, one dominated by doctors, the other containing the other players in health and welfare, meeting only at a very general level of co-ordination or at occasional special events, neither addressing the full implications of interprofessional collaboration. Unless this question is addressed, the professions will all be the losers in a field where policy-makers are looking for solutions to the problem and expense of bridging the gaps in health and welfare.

The search for theory

Two major themes in interprofessional education, even if they are not named in the ostensible titles of courses, are the promotion of teamwork and getting to know more of the knowledge and values, functions and expertise of other professions. The themes are implicit in aims such as improving interpersonal skills, communication, shared problem solving, understanding organisational changes, learning new skills, experiencing and reflecting upon work in small groups. The philosophy underlying courses is frequently that of learning by doing; experiential learning, task-centred, bottom-up planning of programme service orientated, plus a newer emphasis on user-centred involvement and anti-discrimination.

The knowledge base informing these goals, emphasising their relevance to collaborative work, is rarely spelt out. Assumptions are made that given the requirements of practice this knowledge and these skills would be useful. The courses are based on some understanding of competence though that too is rarely spelt out. The assumptions therefore are pragmatic, and interprofessional education remains largely haphazard and localised.

And yet there are bodies of knowledge which could be usefully drawn upon. This knowledge lies mostly in the spheres of the human and social sciences, which to many clinicians are barely respectable and rarely consulted. It is however in theory drawn from studies and understandings of social interaction that illumination of interprofessional collaboration and education may be found. The notion of 'teamwork' could be enriched by studying it in relation to ideas drawn from, for example, social psychology and understanding of intergroup behaviour; Systems Theory and examining the boundaries and interdependence between the team and its environment; sociology and illuminating the roles played and the power balance; social exchange and asking what different people give to and take from the team; social policy and understanding the tasks of the team in relation to the wider arena of health and welfare, and psychology in recognising how team members cope with anxiety in relation to each other and to the patients or clients.

Theory is an explanation independent of the phenomenon being studied, based on principles which are coherent, general and transferable, and of continuing applicability. Without the use of theory, discoveries and understanding remain particular and a body of knowledge does not grow. Unless coherent knowledge grows on which practice and teaching can be based, assessed and evaluated, the enterprise is at the mercy of fashion and expediency.

However, despite the anti-intellectual respectability of the emphasis on service as the main determinant of interprofessional education, and of learning primarily from working together, there are growing numbers of academics and educators who are exploring theoretical understandings of the work and teaching of collaboration. Some of these have affected our understanding of the wider context, some have explored very particular applications for teaching and research, and some have considered interprofessional collaboration directly.

One of the first and most influential publications was that of an occupational sociologist (Huntington 1981) who in studying the occupational structures and cultures of social workers and general practitioners analysed the perceptions and attitudes inhibiting collaboration and hoped by raising awareness to lead to an improvement. She showed that many of the difficulties and frustrations experienced by individuals were rooted in social structures, a perception which perhaps made people feel less personally responsible, but also implied that change would be very difficult. Further analysis from sociology and social policy suggests for example that challenges to the exclusivity and autonomy of professions come not only from the movement for interprofessional collaboration but also from the emphasis on voluntarism and consumerism in the market organisation of the NHS and community care (Carrier and Kendall 1995). This understanding could alert professionals to alternative political agendas in proposals to develop core competencies and core skills.

Several theoretical discussions have drawn upon ideas which have been applied in other programmes but which it is argued might be relevant to the building up of a body of theory for collaborative practice and education. A study of the training and developmental needs of health education professionals put forward a model of the study of work activity based on the relationship of the occupational philosophy, its goals and values, to the practical capability, the competencies and modes of working of the people involved (Rawson 1994). Rawson suggested that mapping overlapping activities would show common elements, sub-sets and shared boundaries in roles and functions, and drew these ideas from Set Theory. He argued that in interprofessional work there is a need for a guiding philosophical framework to avoid pragmatic and purely instrumental thinking and provide the means to assess and evaluate assumptions and contributions.

Another area of work and study which offers transferable concepts is that of health promotion (Beattie 1995). Sociology, anthropology and psychology are drawn upon and Beattie suggests using the metaphor of tribalism to understand institutions and professional cultures. Understanding the power dimension and the negative effects of 'occupational territoriality' would contribute to the evaluation of practice and education. He wonders whether tribalism might lead to new coalitions, or even a new division of labour. This metaphor is also used by Dalley (1989) to suggest that professional ideologies are modified by agency loyalties and circumstances so that new 'tribes' arise, defining afresh who is included and who excluded. She considers that a common identification may be experienced among people of many different professions working in for example the NHS, to define themselves against people working in other agencies and this factor could have a powerful influence on interprofessional harmony.

Collaborative practice and education have themselves been directly studied, using different theoretical perspectives. Evaluating interprofessional education and assessing its effect on participants drawn from medicine, nursing and social work through courses specifically designed on the basis of social psychological studies of intergroup behaviour (Carpenter and Hewstone 1996) found that overall attitudes to others was more positive and knowledge increased.

The importance of understanding one's own inner world and the part played by powerful defences against anxiety is stressed in several approaches to interprofessional collaboration and education using Psychodynamic Theory and allying it with the use of Systems Theory. Substantial work using this combination is carried out within the Tavistock Institute of Human Relations (Obholzer and Roberts 1994). Here work with people in conflict within organisations draws upon an understanding of social systems in the real world and uses psychoanalysis to explore unconscious processes through the use of the self in a structured learning situation to understand that interaction. It is argued that defences employed to avoid pain need to be owned before they can be contained to address conflict and anxiety, and that for multi-professional groups there are problems of the dual membership, of belonging to a home base with a certain culture and certain authority alongside a new grouping raising the issue of a new culture and new sanctioning authority.

Case studies also using the twin approach of Systems Theory and Psychodynamic Theory (Hornby 1993) were drawn upon in an attempt to develop a new language for collaborative care. Hornby suggested that collaboration should be classed as primary or vertical, that is with the client, or secondary or horizontal, that is with others. Defences are to be understood through Psychodynamic Theory, whilst an understanding of Social Systems illustrates structure and boundaries and leads to a holistic perception.

In interprofessional education Psychodynamic Theory is related to the idea of Reflective Practice, developed from the work of Donald Schon (1983). Practitioners know more in their practice than they can acknowledge, it is argued, and to make this knowledge in action accessible, practitioners need to reflect upon their behaviour. Schon uses the metaphor of jazz where musicians listen and improvise within a stable framework of metre and harmony. Such a framework for interprofessional education might be drawn from Psychodynamic Theory (Trowell 1995) so that 'thoughtless action becomes thoughtful'. The theoretical framework makes it possible to confront difference by recognising how powerful and primitive feelings aroused by the nature of the work with pain and need give rise to defences such as splitting, denial and projection which puts all the bad on to others.

Collaborative professional practice is described by writers familiar with community development in social work (Beresford and Trevillion 1995). Their aim is to identify and develop skills for collaboration in community care. The stress is not so much upon knowledge but upon a system of values informing practice in which the user is at the centre of a web of communication, empowered to exercise independence and choice within a needs-led response. This goal, rather than the traditional professional perspective, governs the processes employed and the services offered. The espousal of such values would create a new culture of collaboration.

The assumption behind studies and analyses is that a need is identified in practice; for example, better communication. The appropriate theory, say social psychology, makes sense of the need, so that the response for both practice and education is grounded in a particular and general understanding. Learning is therefore both deductive, that is drawn down from a general body of knowledge, and inductive, that is drawn up from experience, from the particular. The relevance of either is tested by the other. The searches for relevant theory in collaboration have so far been unrelated. The need now is for a coherent framework to inform practice and education.

CHAPTER FIVE

A Conceptual Framework for Collaboration

The introduction offers a definition of collaboration and a summary of the historical assumptions behind it and the mechanisms for promoting it. The emphasis on interprofessional education for individuals is a response to the difficulties in practice but these difficulties are also present in groups, organisations and agencies, which have common social elements.

Discussion of theories of social interaction as they illuminate the key social elements of structures, power and culture leads to the development of a framework for understanding collaboration. This sets out a matrix which, it is argued, might be used to clarify the essential conditions to be considered in setting up, organising, maintaining and evaluating collaborative enterprises. The necessary skills are related to the essential conditions, and core skills are suggested. These are assessment, building, managing the process *and* evaluating, *the emphasis being on the social context of collaboration, both within and around each* enterprise. *Such an emphasis enables the difficulties to be openly addressed at an organisational as well as an individual level. The framework is offered as a basis for both education and practice in interprofessional collaboration.*

Introduction

Collaboration in health and welfare is the acting together of two or more people from different professions either within the same or from different agencies to deliver a service which neither can deliver alone. It requires competence, that is fitness for purpose based on knowledge, skills and attitude, supported by power and authority, structures and resources, and a compatible culture.

Historically it has been assumed to be a rational response to the divided structures of health and welfare, to be a purposive activity aimed at comprehensiveness, despite the division of labour, and to be driven by an altruism which puts the notion of a greater good before sectional interest. In practice, the difficulties often experienced and described witness to irrationality, competition for power and resources, and a defensive holding on to what is known, understood and practised.

Various mechanisms have been tried for developing collaboration and overcoming difficulties, such as exhortation, joint planning and joint funding between health and welfare agencies, statutory requirements and contracting between purchasers representing users' interests making contracts with providers of services. Voluntary organisations have sprung up to co-ordinate and promote collaboration in relation to particular special interests, such as specific illnesses, patient or client groups, or programmes of action such as community or primary health care. A major activity of such bodies has been to pursue and influence interprofessional education, mostly at post-qualifying level as part of continuing education.

Perception of the difficulties as manifesting chiefly through attitudes has led to an emphasis on interprofessional education. This has concentrated on interpersonal skills and the exchange of knowledge between professionals, with the hope of increasing understanding and respect and breaking down mutual stereotypes which are understood as inhibiting collaboration. Working together on real or simulated problems within an educational programme is intended to develop acceptance of the necessity for a range of different contributions if the outcome is to respond to complex situations and to encourage a wider range of collaborative skills and the development of more positive attitudes. On the whole therefore the response to calls for collaboration and to the experience of difficulties has been to concentrate on the education of individuals or of small work-groups. Positive change through education in attitudes and knowledge has been evaluated and identified, but it is also necessary to be realistic and acknowledge that returning changed people to unsupportive environments is not the most effective way of sustaining such change. While knowledge, skills and attitudes are necessary conditions for collaboration they are not sufficient. Education has been the most accessible and least disruptive mechanism for bringing about change but it is not sufficient unless the focus can be widened to include an understanding of structures, of the use and distribution of power and of the purpose and effect of culture. Nor is education sufficient if it is concentrated only on individuals too junior or too powerless to bring about necessary changes in spheres wider than their own immediate practice. Both individual and systemic change are necessary.

The difficulties in collaboration apparent in the behaviour of individuals also pervade groups, organisations and agencies. At these levels the difficulties both arise from and can be perceived in structures, power and culture. These elements are essential features of all groups, organisations and agencies and familiar to anyone working in such bodies. It is these elements which practitioners, educators, managers and policy-makers must explore and understand in relation to collaboration in health and welfare. Without making the effects of these elements explicit and being able to take account of and use them, collaboration cannot become a well-founded, effective and sustained service response to need. The tools for exploring these common elements are to be found in theories of social interaction, because collaboration is interaction, in both its purpose and its processes.

How theories of social interaction illuminate structures, power and culture in relation to collaboration

Some of the theories of social interaction which can be applied to structures, power and culture in social organisations are those of Systems Theory, Social Exchange Theory and Co-operation Theory.

Systems Theory is relevant because it sets out an understanding of complex entities which are both whole in themselves and yet to survive need to relate across open boundaries with other similar entities in a web of interdependence. Social Exchange Theory is relevant because it deals with social transactions

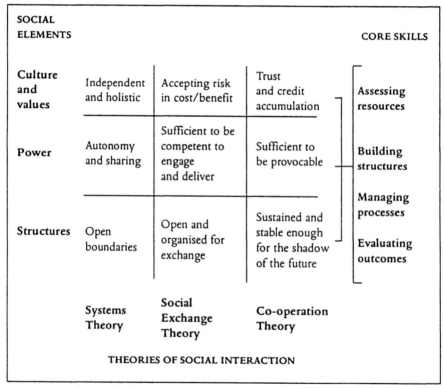

Figure 5.1. A framework for collaboration

involving cost/benefit exchanges which have meanings for the participants beyond the economic. Co-operation Theory is relevant because it argues that in conditions of uncertainty conditional co-operation is the most effective strategy for ensuring overall mutual benefit and gaining trust.

Collaboration involves complex entities which are interdependent. It involves exchanges which might be both costly and beneficial and which carry sophisticated and unquantifiable meanings. It is set in situations of uncertainty and risk where trust is a necessary condition for success. It should be possible to arrive at an understanding of collaboration and the social context in which it is set by taking from these theories of social interaction the concepts which highlight the characteristics of structures, power and culture relevant to collaboration.

In using Systems Theory the key explanation which applies to structures is that to survive energy in the form of information, resources and services has to be exchanged across open boundaries between one system and others coexisting interdependently. Such exchanges take place across both internal and external boundaries and can be tracked by examining how the structure is organised to, for example, communicate information in and out. Within Systems Theory power may be understood because of the interdependence of wholes to be both autonomous and shared, a mixture of both in different proportions according to the particular degree of interdependence. Power is therefore shifting not fixed and is related to what needs are and where the competences are to respond. Systems Theory in emphasising the interdependence of wholes challenges a reductionist, a 'nothing but' view of entities – the fractured femur in the third bed on the left, the inadequate mother, the drug addict. Culture and values which affect frames of reference and attitudes are shown within the context of Systems Theory to depend on a holistic perspective of people.

Social Exchange Theory would suggest that structures need to be so organised that they enable, support and maintain exchanges both internally and externally which might carry both the risks of costs and the hope of gain. Social Exchange Theory points out that participants need sufficient power to be competent to engage and deliver whatever is being exchanged, whether it be goods or services. It is not equal power, but sufficient. If the power is insufficient, then the stronger party could take what it wants without giving anything in exchange. The weaker must have enough power, in terms of resources, skills, credibility and support, to protect itself against exploitation. For example, staff from one agency attached to another need lines of communication and resources from their base agency which make it possible to contribute to the new host from a position of enough strength to be fully included without being sucked in and dominated. Culture and values, within Social Exchange Theory, are permeated with the idea of openness so as to exchange between strengths and deficits in a pattern of interaction which results in a creative balance between costs and benefits.

Co-operation Theory in emphasising the importance for co-operation of 'the shadow of the future', that is the expectation that the parties will meet again and therefore expect either that the relationship will be rewarding or that there could be some retaliation, suggests that structures should be so organised to guarantee future and ongoing contact. In relation to power Co-operation Theory makes it clear that each party needs sufficient power to be provocable and to retaliate if the other cheats on the agreement. It is assumed that each starts out with an expectation of co-operation, but that each is competent to return tit for tat if the other reneges. Culture and values within Co-operation Theory are based on the importance of trust and the slow credit accumulation of trust within society.

The implication for an understanding of collaboration within a social context including structures, power and culture and values is that these elements need to be critically examined within the home bases of the participants, to see how conducive they might be to collaboration. These elements also need to be deliberately built up within collaborative enterprises so that they are sustaining and not disabling.

Structures need to have open boundaries and means of exchanging resources, information and services; they need to be so organised that they are able to take risks in assessing the balance between costs and benefits; they need to be sustained and stable to ensure the 'shadow of the future'; they need to be set up so that they reflect a holistic process, without discontinuities which prevent it, and enable the build-up of trust.

Power is to be recognised as shifting between autonomy and sharing; it does not automatically reside always in the same party but depends on competence in relation to a holistic assessment of needs and the most effective and efficient response. All contributors must have sufficient power to deliver what they promise, which means that not only the collaborative enterprise but also the home base must be committed to engage and to deliver. Power includes competence in terms of knowledge, skills and attitudes as well as in resources both tangible and intangible, such as time; power needs to be sufficiently equal for the parties to be provocable if they are let down, so that parties weaker in status will need to accrue sufficient power from statute, or influence, or expertise, or in agency support, to be credible in retaliation if it is necessary. Power must also include the power not to collaborate – enforced collaboration would not be true collaboration but coercion.

Such coercion would not be true collaboration because it would not be grounded in the culture and values which are illuminated by the theories of social interaction.

A culture for collaboration has an open and holistic perspective which sees people as interdependent in complex situations; the holistic perspective implies that all contributing to an assessment and response have an equal right to be taken seriously, because they are all essential to the whole. The boundaries of the perspective cannot be infinite, otherwise the task would be impossible, but are defined in relation to the desired outcome of the patient or client, the user, who also contributes to the assessment and response. The culture is one which accepts the need to take risks in investing resources and sharing benefits across the boundaries of its own domain. Such risk-taking in collaboration reflects not only the calculation of costs and benefits, profit and loss, but also the emphasis on mutual trust as a necessary component at the start and therefore a possible loss when the participants are unknown, but if collaboration succeeds and trust accumulates, respect and esteem among individuals and agencies becomes a benefit which makes further risk-taking less frightening.

In the cultures of professions and agencies there are embedded values which result in attitudes and frames of reference for action, and no one profession or agency in collaboration in health and welfare would be expected to possess a culture identical to that needed for collaboration. Professions and agencies are not, however, monolithic, and there will be sections among them whose values are sufficiently complementary with sections from other agencies and professions. If collaboration is to succeed, its culture and values need to be explicit and understood so that the parties to collaboration may subscribe to them enough to be willing to work together, to learn the necessary competence and to accept the costs and recognise the benefits.

Skills and processes relevant to the framework for collaboration

Collaborative enterprises need power to combine and act, supported by an enabling structure within a complementary culture, using competent skills and processes. Professionals possessing these need to be competent not only to solve problems, but also to create and maintain collaboration by accruing and using power, building up structures and maintaining the collaborative culture. Such an agenda applies whether collaboration consists of one-off episodes, of loose networks, of liaison or attachment, or of permanent organisations. All these require sanction and power to act, some mandate and agreement on what needs to be done and who is going to do it, information that is understood and passed on, meeting-places and meeting-times, co-ordination and management, to be evaluated and to be accountable. All types of collaboration have the same elements of power, structures and culture and need skills and processes to understand and use them. The process involves *assessment, building, managing the process* and *evaluating*. These are core skills to be within the competence of everyone engaged in collaboration, whatever the profession.

Assessment

The task of assessment is twofold; to reframe the perception of the need so that it provides a common framework for action, and to map the terrain to make apparent the overlaps and gaps in resources, the strengths and the deficits, so that the situation becomes manageable and it is possible to judge and cost the feasibility of collaboration.

Assessment begins with the status of the referral, whether it comes with statutory force, or as a result of contract or particular policies, or because a client or patient sees the agency as appropriate to the ostensible need. Without collaborative skills usually the profession which can define the need or problem in its own terms and within its own frame of reference has got a head start in claiming the patient or client as its own, and determining the contributions of others as supplementary. If the referral comes with the requirement that the need should be met through interprofessional collaboration, then power to collaborate has already been acquired. It is less obvious when an individual chooses an agency, and although collaboration might be the most efficient and effective response, it may not be chosen unless the agency or professional is aware and able to engage it. If collaboration is either required or chosen and the referral has some force, then a main task of assessment is to *reframe the need* so that it is the result of a more comprehensive range of perceptions, and more than bolted-on additions to a dominant definition. Such a reframing provides a common framework for action. It might alter the order of priorities, or emphasise unstated needs, or offer alternative meanings and explanations. This work requires a sharing of power, sufficient understanding of language and terms to communicate effectively, and mutual respect and trust. The more familiar the parties are with each other, providing they share a collaborative culture, the quicker such reframing would be. The patient or client too should be party to the process, though she/he might also need to accept the reframing as other people contribute their perceptions.

The need having been reframed to take account of a holistic perception within the health and welfare system in relation to the user's situation, resources have to be gathered to respond. *Mapping* is a technique which helps to make apparent the overlaps and gaps, the strengths and deficits and the availability of resources so that the situation becomes more manageable and so that the feasibility of the collaborative response can be measured. Who are the participants? What resources do they bring, tangible and intangible? Is there a place? Is there time? Have they relevant skills and knowledge? Do they bring support and resources from their home base? Are they mandated to act? Is power among them sufficiently equal to make provocability if someone reneges a reality – for example, if one professional continually misses key meetings are others able to confront that person and work out together why this is happening and how it might be changed?

Mapping of these factors among the professionals involved in collaboration would show at the start where the strengths and deficits lie in terms of power and structures. If there are too many overlaps of skills and knowledge, then perhaps the number of people involved might be reduced. If there is insufficient support or an inadequate mandate from a member's home base and if it cannot be improved, then that person is not involved. If there is an obvious gap in competence, someone else needs to be recruited. If mapping is carried out at the beginning in a methodical fashion it becomes clear what might be necessary to get started with some chance of success. At the end of this stage in the process it should be apparent who is going to act together. If the collaboration takes place among a loose network this mapping might be done by a small core group, but if it is part of an ongoing organisation it might clarify who actually needs to be involved in any particular situation rather than assuming that everybody is involved every time.

Building

Having assessed the situation so that the need has been reframed to release collaborative action, and the situation mapped to ensure that only effective people and agencies are involved, the next task in relation to power, structures, culture and values is deliberately and specifically to build them. This is necessary so that the collaborative endeavour is deliberately and specifically employed, with the necessary tools and without avoidable handicaps. Boundaries around any group give it an identity which is experienced both by members inside and by the outside world. Without such an identity a collaborative organisation, however small, would not be able to agree goals and deploy resources. Such boundaries are effected by intangible factors like the name, and tangible ones such as place. In building a structure for collaboration and taking into account the elements of power and culture, boundaries need to be open so that information and resources can be exchanged easily and freely within the organisation and between it and the outside – no hurdles to be jumped over, no vacuums into which information disappears.

The organisation needs to be stable and predictable within an agreed time-scale, so that members feel secure, and the 'shadow of the future' has some reality. Structures need to enable and witness to interdependence so that time and place are given enough weight. Are meetings held so that they fit in with other commitments? How much priority and time are members able and willing to give them? Such questions need to be faced openly and negotiated. Place is an important reflection of how power is shared. Is the collaborative enterprise based on a particular territory and if so, whose? Identity and ownership are affected and cannot be ignored. If there is neutral territory available, it means that no one profession appears, particularly to the outside world, to be dominant. The same question applies even to what might seem such a minor factor as whose office meetings are held in. If neutral territory is not available, then meeting-places should be rotated to make sure that power does not unwittingly concentrate in one territory.

Structure also includes the allocation of roles and functions not only in relation to the referral but also within the group. If power is to be acknowledged as shared and if within a holistic perspective everyone is valued and if trust is to build up then negotiation, including renegotiation, is needed to clarify and agree how decisions are to be made by the group and who is to take what roles and when. Roles relate to leadership for particular tasks, including handling meetings, co-ordination of a range of activities, liaison across boundaries with other agencies, managing the flow of information, nurturing the group. The form which the structures and organisation take cannot be prescribed and will depend on each particular group but collaborative principles can be identified and used as a guide.

Relating across the group's boundaries to other agencies is another task for which structures need to be put in place. Lines of communication with significant people outside need establishing, to ensure support and resources. Liaison and network roles have important functions in negotiating and maintaining relationship with outside agencies, especially if such agencies are the home bases for members of the group who may be outposted or attached. The home base gives professional identity and security; for all members of a collaborative group there is a certain role ambiguity, especially if the collaborative values of interdependence and risk-taking seem to threaten the autonomy and domain of the home profession. Structures such as meetings with supportive seniors are essential, particularly for minorities working in a setting secondary to their main base, who may be in danger of colluding or going native within an alien dominant culture and thus failing to make their distinctive contribution to collaboration.

Issues of power and the struggle for power among members of a group are always present and likely to disable collaboration if they are not recognised. Professionals with a higher status in the outside world are likely to assume and be accorded leadership even if their actual competence in particular situations is less than that of other members. Such differentials are not easy to acknowledge, but unless they are acknowledged they cannot be deployed to the benefit of collaboration and may be disabling. If such differentials are exercised within the value framework of interdependence, exchange and trust, it implies a generosity on the part of those with higher status alongside a willingness on the part of others, to accept responsibility so that power and dependence can be flexibly used and experienced. Risk is high at the beginning of collaborative relationships but essential if trust is to build up. The willingness to take such risk needs to be supported by commitment to that particular enterprise and to the general value of collaboration. Accountability to the group for the use of power requires feedback and openness which again are part of the slow build-up of trust.

Managing the process

The progress of the work of collaboration needs to be managed with awareness at three levels. One is in relation to the referral and the desired outcome, the second to the dynamics of the group and the third to ways in which individual members respond to their experience in the situation. As all these processes are managed so the collaborative culture is built up in relation to the structures and use of power.

Communication, whether it is successful or not, is a major measure of whether processes are being successfully managed at all three levels and whether collaborative values are informing what is happening. Is communication within the group open and free? Is it exchanged with equal value being accorded to all members? Are there secrets or is there trust? Communication involves interchange of information and interactions which speak of power, attitudes and values.

The interchange of information which all enquiries into the failures of collaboration have shown to be a major factor has to be consciously organised and managed. Relevance is to be agreed according to the holistic reframing of the perception of the need. The collaborative group needs to decide how data is to be collected, recorded and reported, and how access is to be agreed. Confidentiality is often seen as a major stumbling-block, but information belongs to the client or patient, not the professional, and if the user is involved in the collaborative process, the decision belongs to the user. If for some reason there is information around which is not known to the user, say the details of a prognosis or the attitude of family members, then the professionals need to make a considered judgement of what needs to be withheld and whether it will invalidate the efforts at collaboration. If it does, then collaboration should not proceed. Appeals to professional confidentiality without such openness are a power play.

Information may be exchanged informally but it should be repeated formally so that it may be recorded and conveyed. Formal meetings require clear and agreed agendas, built up to include all perceptions and priorities, a specific focus with agreed goals and allocation of tasks and responsibilities, and to be managed so that all parties take part and contribute to the decisions.

Language in interprofessional collaboration presents a dilemma. It has been argued that specific collaborative terms to be used in common would help (Hornby 1993), or that language sub-sets should be integrated to allow the development of collaborative work (Pietroni 1992) by enabling participants to range widely in reflecting upon practices. The integration necessary to the collaborative process is implemented *between* different professionals, not *in* any one, though to engage at all each needs to be receptive to collaborative principles and values. If a particular language were to be adopted, it would be yet another divisive mechanism which would separate members of a collaborative group from their home bases. Language is a reflection not only of knowledge, but of culture; the word 'patient' carries implications of dependence and authority which are different from the word 'client' which implies the power to engage expertise, and different again from the word 'user' or 'consumer' which implies the freedom to choose in a market. In interprofessional collaboration language, like other elements within culture such as attitude, cannot be taken for granted but must be questioned. All professionals might use the word 'counselling', but the practice would vary depending on the common meaning within each separate profession. It could be sympathetic listening during an extended appointment in a busy surgery, or empathetic responses during the course of physical therapy, or exploration of the meaning of present and past life events over a period of months. Ambiguity needs to be reduced by testing understanding and checking feedback. Diversity of language can enrich if it is acknowledged and if the process of checking it is recognised as needing to be managed.

Messages may be passed not only verbally but also non-verbally in posture, use of eye contact, attitudes of attention or disregard, even practicalities such as choice of seating. In collaborative meetings not only where they are held but how the seating is organised can enable or hinder the process. Can everyone make eye contact? Does anyone sit behind a desk? Has everyone got space? Do people always sit in the same places? Are there enough seats of much the same level of comfort? All these factors give messages about the value placed on interdependence and sharing, and enable or inhibit communication.

Given the referrals coming to collaborative groups which require a complex response there is likely to be some level of anxiety which needs to be dealt with. Anxiety is another word which carries different meanings: to some, admitting it would mean admitting lack of confidence in one's professional competence, to others it is always a component of the situations in which those who need help from professionals find themselves. If anxiety continues over a period of time or is repeatedly aroused it is likely to result in stress. In situations of anxiety and stress professionals commonly employ defence mechanisms such as denial or projection which enable individuals to cope. As discussions of the difficulties in collaboration have repeatedly explored, such defences can work against collaboration. Both groups and individuals to manage themselves require sufficient self-awareness to recognise for example, stereotyping, and the purpose it is serving, and to avoid irritators like always expecting nurses to make tea. The process of managing the situation, the group and one's self will require learned skills, and the greater the distress of the referred situation the more the stress in the group and individuals will need to be acknowledged and supported, even, if necessary, by outside help.

Evaluating

Evaluation of the work directed toward a collaborative response to a referral is a continuous process taking place at every stage, not only at the end. Is the response succeeding, and should understanding of a situation be reframed to take account of new information and new perceptions? A new reframing might lead to a new plan of action and a new agreed goal, a decision to be taken formally by the members of the group. If new resources are needed, either of skills, time, or place, what will they cost, and who will provide them? Costs may not be explicitly financial but may be borne by someone overworking. Their expenditure of skills needs to be recognised and acknowledged.

At the end evaluation needs to assess not only the outcome for the client or patient but also for the collaborative partners, the professionals and the agencies. What costs have been incurred, both tangible and intangible, and what benefits have been gained? Such benefits might include access to a wider range of resources, including a wider range of clients than before or contact with more professionals who can be called upon again in other situations; new knowledge, new skills, the gain of respect or esteem, and the development of trust which builds up a culture of collaboration which will make future working together easier and more quickly effective.

If the costs and benefits can be weighed up so that the benefits to the funding agencies can be demonstrated in terms of present efficiency and client satisfaction then future claims on their resources for collaboration will be strengthened.

Interprofessional practice education and the framework for understanding collaboration

The framework (Figure 5.1) is intended to clarify the necessary conditions for the development of interprofessional collaboration. This is achieved by analysing the organisation of interprofessional collaboration in sociological terms of power, structures, culture and values and relating that analysis to the implications of theories of social interaction. These conditions include interpersonal skills but go beyond them into the social contexts in which they are exercised. It is argued that in attempting to make these contexts explicit, it becomes possible to affect them and deliberately to construct the context for collaboration. The framework is not intended to contain and confine, but to be the basis for construction which is theoretically based, logical and consistent. It provides not a blueprint, but guidelines from which groups may deviate but if they do they do so knowingly. The framework could be a basis for action for example in a contract in setting out what is necessary in advance, so that costs may be estimated and benefits anticipated. It provides guides to strategy in the development of collaboration as well as to tactics in particular situations so that a sufficiently collaborative culture and structures might be established in agencies to make it possible that specific collaborative responses to referrals could be quickly mobilised. The framework clarifies what is necessary across the whole involvement and makes it possible to assess the reality, to identify what has to be accommodated, what might be altered and at what level, to provide the necessary conditions and resources for success, so that it moves interprofessional collaboration from the realm of enthusiasts' hope to a practical proposition, to become not a panacea but a specific application.

Interprofessional education has drawn on ideas of reflective practice, where learning is drawn out at the level of practice. One of the frames of reference which has been used in relation to such reflection is Psychodynamic Theory, which illuminates intra- and inter-personal behaviour. Such a frame is necessary if reflection on practice is to be more than a subjective experience. The framework for collaboration provides yet another basis for reflection in practice and education. Reflection may be reflecting back from someone else, say client or patient; reflecting on what has happened or been done; or reflection from an external source. A framework offers meaning to all these modes and a tool for transferability to other situations thus encouraging innovation and the pursuit of excellence, whether the situations are different but in the same agency, or the same situation in a different agency.

In integrating collaborative theory and practice learning is not linear, but a repetitive spiral. Reflection, assessment and evaluation are important skills to both learning and practice. Learning is inductive, drawing up from practice, and deductive, drawing in from theory. Such learning is not only task-orientated and a specific to the moment, but a widening and deepening of the repertoire of skills and knowledge and attitude to equip the practitioner to respond to the future.

The framework for collaboration does not offer a curriculum, but suggests the questions to which answers must be sought and action related. Those questions are the same ones which practitioners must satisfy. In asking them in education programmes professionals are equipping themselves for practice.

CHAPTER SIX

Conclusion
Values in Collaboration

This final section recapitulates the aim of trying to turn 'collaboration' from either a mystical article of faith or a pragmatic response to gaps in service into an idea which can be understood intellectually, challenged and argued for politically, and turned into practice which addresses the difficulties. The conditions for collaboration set out so far are recognised as necessary, but even together are not sufficient unless attitude is taken into account. Attitude is drawn from values. It is argued that a collaborative culture which knowledge, skills and structures would reflect depends on an essential set of values which makes possible both enrichment from diversity and the reconciliation of difference. A collaborative culture with compatible structures, knowledge and skills together make collaborative practice possible as one way of organising the social task of responding to need in health and welfare.

The evaluation of the idea of collaboration in social policy in health and welfare [see Appendix A] demonstrates how little coherent understanding is apparent. It has been put forward as a desirable expression of social altruism, responding to exhortation; as a necessary bridge over gaps in the organisation of health and welfare, constructed from planning and shifts of resources; as a policy response to limited resources and recognised need, supported by an appeal to a philosophical imperative like community care.

Practitioners from the health and social care professions, and their varied organisations [see Appendix B] have made pragmatic responses to local circumstances, often led by charismatic enthusiasts. The many accounts of difficulties in practice have spurred on attempts to resolve them by education so that interprofessional education is in danger of becoming another untested article of faith.

If interprofessional collaboration in health and welfare, understood as both necessary and difficult, is to become one effective response to social need, it needs to be removed from the realms of aspiration or pragmatism. Through the examination of social policy in the changing conditions of health and welfare since 1970, through consideration of the sources of the difficulties in collaboration as they are manifest in social structures and through the application of social theories of interaction to the social elements of collaborative practice, it has been argued that it should be possible to bring the idea of collaboration into rational discourse.

The notion of holistic care long present in some branches of medicine and therapy and underlying social responses to shared problems is illuminated and enhanced by ideas of working across boundaries, reframing shared perspectives and setting up two-way communication which come from Systems Theory and its applications in practice such as family therapy.

Promoting rationality and reducing the impact of irrationality by clarifying the effects of structures on collaboration complements theories of understanding individual and group behaviour. Collaboration can become purposive in the face of identified difficulties so that it is realistic either to go ahead and address them or to say no.

By recognising the need to balance costs and benefits, and evaluate them in both quantitative and qualitative terms, efficient use of resources can be acknowledged as an essential element in judgement. Resources can be seen as including shared power and information and alliances which reduce the effects of the unknown. Professions able to collaborate and demonstrate integrated care will be better able to challenge such structural responses to social need as carving up skills into new sub-sets which will themselves create more barriers which then have to be overcome.

For interprofessional collaboration to move forward to be defensible, realistic in its ambitions and effective as a specific response, it needs not just empirical study but a theoretical appraisal. This study has been essentially conservative in working from what already exists but also committedly evolutionary, determined not to accept the known difficulties as definitive but to seek tools to move forward and enable the professions to offer an integrated service when it is necessary.

Necessary but insufficient conditions for collaboration

Interprofessional collaboration is a process not of incorporating the knowledge and skills of others but of relating across boundaries given the differences between the professions. It is a device for managing and organising resources, and a technique for delivering services. To succeed, practitioners, managers and policy-makers require sufficient knowledge, a repertoire of relevant skills, appropriate structures for the exchange of information and resources, and processes which facilitate relationships. No one of these alone is sufficient; all are necessary.

Collaboration is recognised as difficult, even risky and dangerous. As well as knowledge, skills, structures and processes it requires trust to work alongside, maybe even to hand over responsibility to, others. This is tricky enough even between people sharing the same profession, with a common training and skills and similar assumptions, but it is very demanding to trust others with a different training, competencies and time-scales, maybe opposing priorities, particularly when these differences are compounded by social differentials. Collaboration is a hard option.

What then is the motivation for interprofessional collaboration? Sometimes it has been argued that it depends on a superordinate goal over and beyond the goals for each professional group but which all can espouse, such as comprehensive services in a locality for a particular population, say drug users. Or it might depend on a policy directive, such as setting up and delivering community care for frail elderly people. Such motivators come from outside, and use collaboration rather than being rooted in it.

Among the necessary conditions which professional education acknowledges is attitude. It stands alongside knowledge and skills and interacts with them and with structures and processes. Attitude is part of culture and reflects values. Values affect not only initial motivation but also the ability to sustain effort even when it is difficult. It has been suggested (Funnell, Gill and Ling 1992) that what people need is to learn to share. Such an ability might be taught through behaviour modification, demonstrating rewards through relating cause and effect, but it might already be present in the values held by individuals who don't need to learn it but just to realise its relevance to collaboration. Collaboration is more than an organisational device, more than a repertoire of techniques. It carries meanings and values for users, clients and patients, professionals, managers and policy-makers and in the wider society.

Values and purposes

Culture is composed of values and beliefs and is expressed through attitudes. Organisations and groups are permeated either explicitly in mission statements or implicitly in assumptions and behaviour with their particular culture. A collaborative culture cannot be taken for granted but needs to be created and developed in the same way that collaborative structures and processes need to be built. The knowledge and skills which are held in common by professionals and agencies engaging in collaboration are the core skills and knowledge and attitudes which deliberately facilitate collaboration, together with the profession specific knowledge, skills and attitudes which contribute to the holistic response to the complex needs of individuals and social groups.

The core values which are essential not because they are ideals but because they are utilitarian and without which collaboration cannot succeed are trust and sharing; these values affect the willingness to engage with different others and they inform the building of structures and the management of processes [Figure 5.1]. The theories of social interaction argue that such values can be developed. As people experience rewarding exchanges and successful co-operation they find that their willingness to take risks is worthwhile, thus building firmer foundations for future engagement.

Trust implies having confidence in others' good faith and being able to rely on their competence. With unknown people there is risk because there is no experience of certainty that giving up some degree of autonomy to them will bring about desirable outcomes. Each situation therefore has to be monitored and tested to make sure that trust is safe. If others prove untrustworthy, trust is not to be unconditional. Trust is however two-way. It implies accepting the responsibility of being worthy of the confidence placed in one but this also emphasises clarity about mutual expectations.

Sharing involves the self-awareness that any one contribution to complex responses to complex needs is only part of what is necessary. Sharing rejects the arrogance which claims pre-eminence. It is also two-way and implies the willingness to contribute and to receive the contributions of others.

The ability to value trust and sharing depends on the confidence which comes from being secure in one's own knowledge, skills and role, so that it is safe to open up without being afraid of being diminished or exploited. This argues that while collaborative skills and knowledge might be taught early in professional training so that they are seen as essential components of a professional repertoire, the attitudes and values on which interprofessional collaboration depends can only be present after professional identity has developed and the participants feel safe.

If trust and sharing are not just desirable but utilitarian in collaboration the outcomes which depend on them need to be identified so that collaboration may be recognised as one efficient response to need. It is efficient because it reduces the impact of unknown knowledge and unknown factors and increases reliability by framing a holistic perception of a situation and ensuring communication across boundaries. Interprofessional collaboration reduces waste and frustration because it enables a wider understanding of meanings in health and social care, for example the patient who rejects prosthesis after prosthesis for an amputated leg because he hasn't come to terms with his loss and changed body image and who needs skilled social work counselling so that he can move on and make use of the skills of the orthopaedic surgeons, the physiotherapists and the technicians.

The processes of collaboration built on trust and sharing recognise the difficulties of interprofessional work, but anticipate them by creating structures and processes which disarm and contain them, so reducing defensiveness, tolerating anxieties and preventing disabling responses such as projection and stereotyping which encourage wasteful enmities. Recognising the part played in the development of collaborative services by building stable and sustained structures reduces failure, wasted effort and disappointment and means that pragmatic enterprises are not continually reinventing the wheel, but can be based on a coherent foundation of knowledge, skills and values. Doing this makes arguing for resources more feasible and accountable, and identifying rewards such as an increased network of resources among people who respect each other more possible.

Trust and sharing enter into the relationship with the user, the client or patient whose needs the collaborative enterprise is intended to meet (Beresford and Trevillion 1995). The emphasis on the role of the user in framing the problem perception, evaluating the outcomes and being part of the processes ensures that collaboration is not a comfortable collusion among known colleagues, but a specific, mobilised response which is accountable, if not directly to the user, to a proxy.

While values in collaboration have an essential function in determining success they are not just utilitarian. Collaboration is both a political and a moral activity in society. It is conditioned by its social context in which it is an actor and with which its participants must engage, if only to affect decisions, influence priorities and accrue resources in competition with others. It is therefore inescapably political.

Equally, it is a moral enterprise and not just a technique or a device. It does not take place in a moral vacuum but in a society which makes assumptions and builds programmes upon them. Collaboration, the idea that working collectively is not only in certain instances more efficient than working separately but also a way of co-operating through which there is a credit accumulation of trust in society, even if only in small clusters, challenges the ethos of self-serving individualism and the pursuit of short-term gain. Collaboration built on a culture of trust, sharing and risk-taking, with compatible structures and complementary processes, providing it is specific and held accountable, works against monopoly and the domination of any one interest. Collaboration witnesses to interdependence and makes it possible to tolerate ambiguity. It therefore either works with or challenges prevailing values in society. It is here that the imperative to collaborate is to be found.

At the beginning of this book the word 'collaboration' rather than 'co-operation' was chosen because of its hint of enmity, hostility and the other. As the discussion has progressed 'collaboration' still seems the right word, but its meaning has expanded. Collaborators may have been wartime traitors, but they may also be colleagues in an artistic endeavour, together creating a new synthesis. Difference relating creatively to difference sparks off a new growth rooted in the differences but developed beyond them. Interprofessional collaboration is only one way of organising the social task of responding to health and welfare needs, but it is value-laden. It reconciles differences to release the richness of diversity, mediated by purposive knowledge, skills and attitudes.

Government Acts and Public Reports Setting Out the Purposes, Mechanisms and Strategies of Collaboration

Document	Purposes	Mechanisms and Strategies
1971 *Better Services for the Mentally Handicapped* DHSS Cmnd. 4683	To provide services to meet the full range of needs	• Exhortation • Good will • Good practice
1973 *Report of the Working Party on Collaboration between the NHS and Local Government* DHSS	• To meet mutual concerns and needs • Comprehensive care • Ensure effective and efficient use of resources • Mutual benefit.	• Planning for provision of closely related services • Forge effective links • Foster close understanding • Share facilities • Staff allocated by skills, making clear the need to co-operate • Conterminosity • Need statutory guidelines.
1973 The National Health Service Reorganisation Act	To secure the health and welfare of the people of their areas	Joint consultation committee, with the statutory obligation to: • co-ordinate allocation of resources • consider policy interaction • co-operate in the exercise of their respective functions.

Document	Purposes	Mechanisms and Strategies
1976 *Joint Care Planning* DHSS (HC 76) 18 (LAC 76) 6	• Develop community-based services to keep people out of hospital • Interdependent balanced services • Effective overall deployment of resources • Essential rationalisation and redevelopment leading to compensating savings to finance development.	• Joint care planning teams – strategic rather than operational • Equal commitment • Joint finance to ease short-term difficulties.
1976 *Fit for the Future* Court Report	Integrated child health services	Multi-disciplinary teams
1977 NHS Act	• Improve co-operation • Make clients aware of the services	Statutory duty to co-operate
1978 *Collaboration in Community Care* Personal Social Services Council, Central Health Services Council	Collaboration	• Better communication • Joint training • Multi-disciplinary working • Develop agreed procedures to identify purpose, form, and resource implications of development.
1979 Jay Report on *Mental Handicap Nursing and Care*	Comprehensive service, meeting needs	Shared training
1979 *Royal Commission on the NHS* DHSS Cmnd. 7615	• Encourage closer working relationships • Establish effective collaboration without structural merging.	• Determination and positive attitudes • Appropriate training • Staff with authority in own organisation, continuity in post, and educated in the importance of interprofessional collaboration.

Document	Purposes	Mechanisms and Strategies
1979 *Patients First* DHSS	• Responsive to needs • Overcome lack of support for suggestions of transferring services – the NHS to local government, social services to the NHS, family practitioner committees to health authorities.	• Will to work together • Administer joint finance projects together.
1981 *Care in Action* DHSS	• Broad spectrum of care includes voluntary and private as well as statutory services • A common challenge – best services within limits of resources.	• Ministerial dictat 'I want to see as close collaboration as possible' • Addressed to both health authorities and social service committees • Identify priority groups • Identify priority services.
1981 *Care in the Community* DHSS	Sharing resources	More flexible use of resources
1982 *NHS Restructuring Collaboration between the NHS and Local Government* DHSS	• Responsive to need • Cost effective.	• Local decision-making • Simplicity a principle in setting up collaborative committees • Joint care for priority groups and services.
1983 *Care in the Community and Joint Finance* HC (86) 6 DHSS	• Community care • Preventative medicine • Services for priority groups.	Joint finance – direct payments from health authorities – time limits and tapering extended

Document	Purposes	Mechanisms and Strategies
1984 *Report of the Working Group on Collaboration between Family Practitioner Committees and District Health Authorities* DHSS	• Closer working partnerships to serve the interests of the community • Secure co-operation • Rationalisation of services and resources • Health promotion	• Identify aims and principles of collaboration-mutual understanding and respect for each other's role and responsibility • Encourage people to plan and work together • Agreements for sharing information • Identify areas of common interest and concern • Establish and pursue common goals, policies and programmes • Separate structures • Formal arrangements and informal links by simplest means and at levels appropriate to functions.
1985 House of Commons *Second Report from Social Services Committee on Community Care*, with reference to the adult, mentally ill and mentally handicapped people	• Maintain present degree of integration between social services and other local authority services • Priority of NHS and local authority to mandatory services • Match rhetoric with action • Services in the community • Individual care plans.	• Joint care planning depends on a sense that all those involved are in the same business • Permanent staff • Participation of senior officers • Greater financial and policy autonomy • Assurance of full information • Realism through specifying priorities and phasing work • Joint Consultative Committee present reports for DHSS and regional health authority monitoring.
1986 *NHS Training Authority* DHSS	Meet corporate objectives	Training

Document	Purposes	Mechanisms and Strategies
1986 NHS – Health Pickup DHSS	• Deal with health care issues • Crossing professional boundaries.	Teamwork
1986 Progress in Partnership – Report of Working Group on Joint Planning Local Authority Association and National Association of Health Authorities	• Collaboration • Develop services for priority groups • Improve use of resources • Produce right mix of services • Avoid gaps in duplication.	• Resources • Consultation • Structures • Accountability • Balanced teams, and no separate teams • Training in joint planning and working at all levels • Key appointments for programming and co-ordinating • Interactive process, neither bottom-up nor top-down.
1986 Collaboration between the NHS, Local Government and Voluntary Organisations DHSS	• Effective and economical meeting of each person's individual needs • Follow government strategy for developing community-based services.	• Joint planning • Regional health authorities monitor, review and assess • Informal links, members and officers • Consultation forum • Leadership from Joint Consultative Committee • Annual report to Minister • Wide use of resources.
1986 Green Paper on Primary Health Care DHSS Cmnd. 9771	• Dependence of health care on co-operation • Realising full potential • Best use of resources • More effective use of skills and knowledge.	• Teamwork • Separate structures give place as of right 'at the planning table', that is, collaborate on equal terms with other agencies.
1986 Neighbourhood Nursing – A Focus for Care Cumberlege Report	• Comprehensive care • Fuller use of skills • Job satisfaction.	Formal agreements

Document	Purposes	Mechanisms and Strategies
1987 *Primary Health Care* House of Commons Select Committee on Social Services	• Development of multi-disciplinary services extending beyond boundaries of NHS • In long run, amalgamation of health authorities and family practitioner committees • Prevention and promotion • Meeting needs of populations served.	• Improvements in co-operation and teamwork • Core written agreements • Multi-disciplinary training in promoting teamwork, management of the primary health care team, making all health professionals aware of their respective responsibilities and skills • Encouragement from government for learning to work together • Arrangements for some social workers to work from the same premises as the general practitioners • Identify appropriate member of team to extend preventative work.
1987 *Promoting Better Health* DHSS Cmnd. 249	• Services responsive to needs of the consumer • Raise standards of care • Promote health and prevent illness • Give patients widest range of choice • Value for money • Clearer priorities for family practitioner services	• Increase fair and open competition • Consumer access to information • Remuneration limited to performance • Cost-effective targeting of resources available • Encourage effective collaboration with other agencies – review collaboration

Document	Purposes	Mechanisms and Strategies
1990 NHS and Community Care Act	• Separate purchasers from providers and require them to work through contracts • Make possible agency arrangements between local authorities and other bodies for accommodation and welfare services.	• In community care the local authority to assess needs, plan for the provision of services • The local authority has the responsibility to consult, notify and invite to assist the DHA, FHSA, Housing Department and voluntary organisations if either the assessment or the provision is likely to involve them.

United Kingdom National Co-Ordinating Bodies Promoting Shared Working

Name	Aims/Purpose	Membership	Activities
Centre for the Advancement of Interprofessional Education Primary Health and Community Care, founded 1987.	To promote high quality developments in practice and research in interprofessional education and training in primary health and social care.	Individual and organisational from educators, advisers, researchers, managers from medicine, nursing, social work and professions allied to medicine.	Databases, publications, conferences, seminars, research, regional networks lobbying and representation.
INTERACT (Scotland), founded 1987	To provide an interdisciplinary forum for consideration of major issues in health and social care fields.	Informal grouping of health and social care professionals.	Mailing list, networking, conferences.
Anticipatory Care Teams, ACT, started 1987.	To promote teamworking in primary care to improve the health of the population.	Membership from large database of those working in primary health care.	Conferences, resource materials.
Health and Care Professions Education Forum, founded 1989.	Forum to share common concerns and develop perspectives on multi-professional health and social care.	BDA, BOS, BPS, CCETSW, CSP, C of R, COT, C of SLT, ENB, IBS, SCP. (see glossary)	Organises conferences; produces a directory of educational institutions of professions allied to medicine.

Name	Aims/Purpose	Membership	Activities
National Primary Care Facilitation Programme, started 1990.	To develop the role of the primary facilitator through support and education.	Some 227 facilitators and associated organisations.	Newsletter, resources, database, training events, publicity and promotion.
Continuing Care at Home, CONCAH, founded 1991.	To improve services by raising awareness of problems and needs and improving interprofessional collaboration.	Individual and institutional.	Encourages local activities, runs workshops, organises conferences and seminars, publishes newsletters and publications.
The Alliance of Primary Care, founded 1992.	Share information about member activities: act together on matters of shared interest: improve co-ordination at national level.	AMGP, CNA, CAIPE, BMA, HVA, NAHAT, RCGP, RCM, RCN, ADSS invited. (see glossary)	Shares information, comments jointly on relevant interests, campaigns and lobbies.
RCGP Commission on Primary Care, founded 1992	Educational remit: improve services through better interprofessional work facilitated by learning together locally.	RCGP members and educators from AMGP, CAIPE, CNA, CCETSW, HVA, Osteopaths, NHSTD, Patients Liaison Group, RCM, RCN, South Bank University. (see glossary)	Five Educational Fellowships to promote multi-professional teamwork locally for learning disability, physical disability, mental health, children, the elderly.
Health Education Authority Primary Health Care Unit, started 1992.	Supports local organising teams by providing workshops, focused on health promotion.	Members active in health promotion – facilitators, general practitioners, district or practice nurses, staff from FHSA/HA/SSDs	Newsletter: training courses, resource materials.

Name	Aims/Purposes	Membership	Activities
Standing Conference on Public Health, founded 1992.	Alliance of health and social care professions to promote action, research, training, multi-disciplinary education, to disseminate knowledge and good practice in public health.	ACHC, Association for Public Health, BDA, BPS, HVA, Institute of Environmental Health Officers, IHSM, NCVO, NISW, RCGP, RCN, Royal Society of Health, Society of Public Health, RIPHH. (see glossary)	Campaigns and lobbies on issues, writing groups, educational materials and information.

Reproduced and adapted with permission from CAIPE, January 1996.

List of Acronyms

ACHC	Association of Community Health Councils
ACT	Anticipatory Care Teams
ADSS	Association of Directors of Social Work
AMGP	Association of Managers in General Practice
BDA	British Dietetic Association
BDA	British Dental Association
BMA	British Medical Association
BOS	British Orthoptic Society
BPS	British Psychological Society
CAIPE	Centre for the Advancement of Interprofessional Education
CCETSW	Central Council for Education and Training in Social Work
CHCs	Community Health Councils
CNA	Carers National Association
COT	College of Occupational Therapists
C of R	College of Radiographers
C of SLT	College of Speech & Language Therapists
CSP	Chartered Society of Physiotherapy
ENB	English National Board for Nursing, Midwifery & Health Visiting
FHSA	Family Health Services Authority
HA	Health Authority
HEA	Health Education Authority
HVA	Health Visitors Association
IBS	Institute of Biomedical Science
IHSM	Institute of Health Service Managers
NAHAT	National Association of Health Authorities and Trusts

NCVO   National Council of Voluntary Organisations
NHSTD   NHS Training Directorate
NISW   National Institute of Social Work
RCGP   Royal College of General Practitioners
RCM   Royal College of Midwives
RCN   Royal College of Nursing
RCP   Royal College of Physicians
RIPHH   Royal Institute of Public Health & Hygiene
SCP   Society of Chiropodists & Podiatrists
SSDs   Social Services Departments

Reproduced and adapted with permission from CAIPE, January 1996

References

Aaron, H. J. and Schwartz, W. B. (1984) *The Painful Prescription: Rationing Hospital Care.* The Brookings Institution.

Alsopp, J. (1984) *Health Policy and the NHS.* London: Longman.

Audit Commission (1986) *Report on Community Care.* London: HMSO.

Audit Commission (1992) *Community Care: Managing the Cascade of Change.* London: HMSO.

Axelrod, R. (1984) *The Evolution of Co-operation.* New York: Basic Books, Inc.

Barr, H. (1994) 'NVQs and their implications for interprofessional collaboration.' In A. Leathard (ed) *Going Interprofessional – Working Together for Health and Welfare.* London: Routledge.

Barr, H. and Waterton, S. (1996) *Interprofessional Education in Health and Social Care – The Report of a United Kingdom Survey.* London: CAIPE.

Beattie, A. (1995) 'War and peace among the health tribes.' In K. Soothill, L. MacKay and C. Webb (eds) *Interprofessional Relations in Health Care* London: Edward Arnold.

Bennett, P., Dewar, A. and Dick, A (1972) 'Interprofessional co-operation.' *Journal of the Royal College of General Practitioners* 22, 603–609.

Beresford, P. and Trevillion, S. (1995) *Developing Skills for Community Care: a Collaborative Approach.* Aldershot: Arena.

Bertalanffy, L. von (1971) *General Systems Theory.* London: Allen Lane, The Penguin Press.

Bell (1986) Unpublished student research dissertation.

Bolman, L. G. and Deal, T. E. (1984) *Modern Approaches to Understanding and Managing Organisations.* New York: Jossey-Bass Inc.

Bond, J. *et al.* (1985) *A Study of Interprofessional Collaboration in Primary Health Care Organisations. Vol. 1* Summary Health Care Research Unit, University of Newcastle upon Tyne.

Brieland, D., Briggs, T. and Levenberger, P. (1973) *The Team Model of Social Work Practice* Manpower Monograph Number Five. New York: Syracuse University.

Bulmer, M. (1986) *Neighbours: The Work of Philip Abrams.* Cambridge: Cambridge University Press.

Bywaters, P. (1986) 'Social work and the medical profession – arguments against unconditional collaboration.' *British Medical Journal of Social Work* 16, 661–677.

Bywaters, P. (1989) 'Social work and nursing: sisters or rivals?' In R. Taylor and J. Ford (eds) *Social Work and Health Care* London: Jessica Kingsley Publishers.

Carpenter, J. and Hewstone, M. (1996) 'Shared learning for doctors and social workers: an evaluation.' *British Journal of Social Work 26*, 2, April, 239–257.

Carrier, J. and Kendall, I. (1995) 'Professionalism and interprofessionalism in health and community care: Some theoretical issues.' In P. Owens, J. Carrier and J. Horder (eds) *Interprofessional Issues in Community and Primary Health Care.* London: Macmillan.

Challis, L. *et al.* (1988) *Joint Approaches to Social Policy.* Cambridge: Cambridge University Press.

Clare, A. W. and Corney, R. H. (eds) (1982) *Social Work and Primary Health Care.* London: Academic Press.

Cohen, A. (1995) 'The Market and professional frameworks.' In P. Owens, J. Carrier and J. Horder (eds) *Interprofessional Issues in Community and Primary Health Care.* London: Macmillan.

Collins, J. (1965) *Social Casework in a General Medical Practice.* London: Pitman.

Court Report (1976) *Fit for the Future.* London: HMSO.

Cumberlege Report (1986) *Neighbourhood Nursing: A Focus for Care.* London: HMSO.

Dalley, G. (1989) 'Professional ideology or organisational tribalism? The health service – social work divide.' In R. Taylor and J. Ford (eds) *Social Work and Health Care.* London: Jessica Kingsley Publishers.

Dartington, T. (1986) *The Limits of Altruism.* London: King's Fund.

Davidson, K. and Clark, S. (eds) (1990) *Social Work in Health Care.* New York and London: The Haworth Press.

DHSS (1971) *Better Services for the Mentally Handicapped.* Cmnd. 4683. London: HMSO.

DHSS (1973) *Report of the Working Party on Collaboration between the NHS and Local Government* London: HMSO.

DHSS (1974) *Annual Report of the Department of Health and Social Security 1974.* London: HMSO.

DHSS (1976) *Joint Care Planning.* (HC76)18 (LAC76)6. London: DHSS.

DHSS (1979a) *Royal Commission on the NHS.* Cmnd. 7615. London: HMSO.

DHSS (1979b) *Patients First.* London: HMSO.

DHSS (1981a) *Care in Action.* London: HMSO.

DHSS (1981b) *Care in the Community.* London: HMSO.

DHSS (1982) *NHS Restructuring: Collaboration between the NHS and the Local Government.* London: HMSO.

DHSS (1983) *Care in the Community and Joint Finance.* HC(86)6. London: DHSS.

DHSS (1984) *Report of the Joint Working Group on Collaboration between Family Practitioner Committees and District Health Authorities.* London: HMSO.

DHSS (1986a) *NHS Training Authority.* London: HMSO.

DHSS (1986b) *NHS – Health Pick Up.* London: HMSO.

DHSS (1986c) *Collaboration between the NHS, Local Government and Voluntary Organisations.* London: HMSO.

DHSS (1986d) *Green Paper on Primary Health Care.* Cmnd. 9771. London: HMSO.

DHSS (1987) *Promoting Better Health.* Cmnd. 249. London: HMSO.

Dubos, R. (1979) *Mirage of Health.* New York: Harper.

Engel, G. L. (1977) 'The need for a new medical model: a challenge for biomedicine.' *Science 196,* 4286, 129–135.

Faculty of Community Medicine (1985) *Health for All by the Year 2000.* London: Royal College of Physicians.

Flack, G. (1980) 'The symposium on interprofessional learning.' In H. England *Education for Co-operation in Health and Social Work.* Occasional Paper 14, RCGP.

Friedson, E. (1970) *Profession of Medicine: A Study in the Sociology of Applied Knowledge.* New York: Dodd Mead.

Funnell P, Gill, J. and Ling, J. (1992) 'Competence through interprofessional shared learning.' In *Aspects of Educational Technology Vol XXV, Developing and Measuring Competence,* 3–7. London: Kogan Page.

Godber, G. (1975) *The Health Service: Past, Present and Future.* London: University of London/The Athlone Press.

Griffiths Report (1988) *Community Care: Agenda for Action.* London: HMSO.

HMSO (1996) *Social Trends 25 1995 Edition.* Government Statistical Service. London: HMSO.

Horder, J. (1994) 'Dr Ekke Kvenssberg CBE, a tribute.' *CAIPE Bulletin 7,* 9.

Horder, J. (1995) Continuing Education in Primary Care: summary of a report on a meeting at RCGP, 9.6.94. *CAIPE Bulletin 9,* 15–16.

Hornby, S. (1993) *Collaborative Care – Interprofessional, Interagency and Interpersonal.* Oxford: Blackwell.

House of Commons (1985) *Second Report from Social Services Committee on Community Care.* London: House of Commons.

House of Commons (1987) *Primary Health Care.* Report from Select Committee on Social Services. London: House of Commons.

Huntington, J. (1981) *Social Work and General Medical Practice.* London: George Allen and Unwin.

Huntington, J. (1986) The proper contributions of social workers in health practice. *Soc Sci Med 22* 11, 1151–1160.

Hutton, W. (1995) *The State We're In.* London: Jonathon Cape.

Illich, I. (1975) *Limits to Medicine: Medical Nemesis, the Expropriation of Health.* London: Boyars.

Jay Report (1979) *Mental Handicap Nursing and Care.* London: HMSO.

Jenkins, D. E. (1990) *The Market and Health Care.* Occasional Paper No.19. Edinburgh: Centre for Theological and Public Issues, University of Edinburgh.

Leathard, A. (ed) (1994) *Going Interprofessional – Working Together for Health and Welfare.* London: Routledge.

Local Authorities Association and National Association of Health Authorities (1986) *Progress in Partnership ... Report of Working Group on Joint Planning.* London: LAA and NAHA.

Loxley, A. (1980) 'A study of multi-disciplinary in-service training in the interests of health care.' *Social Work Service 9,* 1980 35–43.

Loxley. A. (1984) 'Educating the educators.' Enfield: Middlesex Polytechnic (unpublished report).

McKeown, T. (1976) *The Role of Medicine: Dream, Mirage or Nemesis?* Oxford: Nuffield Provincial Hospitals Trust/Basil Blackwell.

National Health Service Reorganisation Act (1973) London: HMSO.

NHS Act (1977) London: HMSO.

NHS and Community Care Act (1990) London: HMSO.

Navarro, V. (1977) *Health and Medical Care in the US.* New York: Baywood Publishing Co Ltd.

Obholzer, A. and Roberts, V. Z. (1994) *The Unconscious at Work: Individual and Organisational Stress in the Human Services.* London: Routledge.

Pearson, G., Gilman, M. and McIver, S. (1985) *Young People and Heroin: An Examination of Heroin Use in the North of England.* Research Report No. 8. Health Education Council.

Pereira Gray, D. *et al.* (1993) 'Multi-professional education at the Postgraduate Medical School, University of Exeter, United Kingdom.' *Annals of Community-Orientated Education 6,* 181–190.

Personal Social Services Council and Central Health Services Council (1978) *Collaboration in Community Care.* London: PSSC.

Pietroni, M. (1991) 'Right or Privilege? Post-qualifying training with special reference to child care'. *Collected Papers from a Writing Group, Study 10.* London: CCETSW.

Pietroni, M. (1992) 'Towards reflective practice – the languages of health and social care.' *Journal of Interprofessional Care 6,* 1, 7–16.

Pincus, A. and Minahan, A. (1973) *Social Work Practice: Model and Method.* Illinois: F. E. Peacock Publishers Inc.

Platt, D. (1995) 'Then, now, onwards – social work centenary public lecture.' *Professional Social Work, Dec. 1995,* 8–9.

PSI (1991) *Britain in 2010 Policy Studies Institute Report.* London: PSI.

Rawson, D. (1994) Models of interprofessional work – likely theories and possibilities. In A. Leathard (ed) *Going Interprofessional – Working Together for Health and Welfare.* London: Routledge.

Renshaw, J. *et al.* (1988) *Care in the Community: The First Steps.* London: Gower Publishing Co Ltd.

Rogers, J. (1995) NHS Executive, Human Resources Division. Address to CAIPE AGM 1995. *CAIPE Bulletin 10,* 2 and 3.

Ross, S. and Bilson, A. (1989) *Social Work Management and Practice.* London: Jessica Kingsley Publishers

Saks, M. (1995) *Professions and the Public Interest: Medical Power, Altruism and Alternative Medicine.* London: Routledge.

Savage, W. (1986) *A Savage Enquiry.* London: Virago Press.

Schon, D. A. (1983) *The Reflective Practitioner: How Professionals Think in Action.* New York: Basic Books.

Schon, D. A. (1991) 'Reflective practice and phenomenology'. In *Interprofessional Collaboration: The Vision and the Challenge.* A conference organised by CAIPE, the Marylebone Centre and the King's Fund, June 1991.

Seebohm, F. (1968) *Report of the Committee on Local Authority and Allied Personal Services* (Cmnd 3703). London: HMSO.

Shakespeare, H. *et al.* (1989) *Report of a National Survey on Interprofessional Education in Primary Health Care.* London: Institute of Community Studies.

Smith, R. (1993) 'Helpers in harmony.' *Community Care April.* 25–26.

Stacey, M. (1988) *The Sociology of Health and Healing.* London: Unwin Hyman.

Storrie, J. (1992) 'Mastering interprofessionalism – an enquiry into the development of Masters Programmes with an interprofessional focus.' *Journal of Interprofessional Care 6,* 3.

Taylor, R. and Ford, J. (eds) (1989) *Social Work and Health Care.* London: Jessica Kingsley Publishers.

Thwaites, M. (1993) 'Interprofessional training: a brief history.' *CAIPE Bulletin 6,* 2–3.

Timmins, N. (1995) *The Five Giants – a Biography of the Welfare State.* London: Harper Collins.

Titmuss, R. (1970) *The Gift Relationship.* London: George Allen and Unwin.

Townsend, P. and Davidson, N. (eds) (1982) *Inequalities in Health: The Black Report.* Harmondsworth: Penguin.

Trowell, J. (1995) 'Working together in child protection: some issues for training from a psychodynamic perspective.' In M. Yelloly and M. Henkel (eds) *Learning and Teaching in Social Work – Towards Reflective Practice.* London: Jessica Kingsley Publishers.

WHO (1978) *Report of the International Conference on Primary Healthcare, Alma Ata, USSR, 6–12 September 1978*. Geneva: WHO.

WHO Study Group on Multiprofessional Education (1988) 'Learning together to work together for health. The team approach.' *WHO Technical Report Series 769*. Geneva: WHO.

United Kingdom Central Council (1986) *Project 2000 – A New Preparation for Practice*. London: UKCC.

Subject Index

Adult Learning, *see* Education

altruism/altruistic, 8, 40, 76

anxiety, 22, 86

assessing/assessment, vii, 76, 78, 81–83, 88

attitude, 18, 19, 20, 40, 77, 91

building, 3, 34, 41, 76, 78, 81, 83–85

clients, *see* users

collaboration, vii, 1, 39, 42
  attitudes in, 18, 19, 40
  benefits of, 40, 45
  categories of, 17
  conditions for, 22, 39, 76, 77, 87–88, 90
  costs of, 2, 37, 40, 42, 45, 46–47
  criteria for, 47
  culture of, 75, 76–88
  dangers of, 42–47
  definitions of, 1, 5, 25, 37, 50, 76, 78, 91, 93–94
  development of, 64–66
  difficulties in, vii, 2, 3, 18, 48–49, 63, 76, 77
  education for, 66–69, 72
  framework for, 1, 24–25, 36, 76–88

history of, 4–23, 76–77

inter-agency, vii, viii, 14, 42

inter-professional, vii, viii, 14, 42, 90

knowledge for, 24–25, 40

mechanisms for, 18, 19, 77, 95–101

organisations supporting, 3, 102–104

philosophy of, 15, 22

power in, 18, 76–88

principles of, 20

process in, 2, 81–87, 90, 93

purposes of, 2, 4, 45, 92, 95–101

reflection on, 21, 88

skills in, 19, 25, 41, 76, 78, 81–88

social policy for, 4–23, 95–101

strategies for, 95–101

structures for, 2, 9, 17, 19, 76–88

theory for, 2, 25, 34–40, 72–75, 78–81

tools for, 17–21, 76–88

values in 3, 76–88, 89–94

communication, 90
  collaboration and, 85–87, 92
  non-verbal, 86
  structures for, 85
  verbal, 85–86

Community Care, 28, 37, 39, 60, 77, 89
  costs, 19, 61
  lead agency, 16, 18, 29
  managers, 14, 39
  policy, 8, 16, 32, 42

values in, 27, 75

community nurses, *see* nursing

competition, *see* markets

consumers, *see* users

contract, *see* market

co-operation, 1, 11, 37
  Co-operation Theory, 34, 38–40, 78–81

co-ordination, 4, 8, 32, 33
  in teamwork 69, 70

core skills/worker, *see* generic

counselling/counsellors, 21, 56, 70, 86

culture,
  collaborative 75, 76
  concept of, 2, 48, 50, 77, 78–81, 91
  occupational, 55–59, 73
  professional, 43, 58–59

defences, 55, 57, 74, 86

difference, 2, 43, 44, 48–75
  differential, 43, 50, 84
  differentiation, 62–63
  social, 1, 2

district nurses, *see* nursing

division of labour, 1, 2, 11, 76
  development in health and welfare 32–34, 49–50, 62–63
  specialisms in, 68

education/educators, vii, 3, 20, 78
  Adult Learning, 71
  curriculum, 88
  growth in, 3, 66–69

Names Index

Printed in the United Kingdom
by Lightning Source UK Ltd.
124136UK00001B/274-282/A